MIDNIGHT ON THE DESERT

J. B. Priestley

FICTION

Adam in Moonshine · Benighted · The Old Dark House · Faraway · Farthing Hall (with Hugh Walpole) · I'll Tell You Everything (with Gerald Bullett) The Good Companions · The Town Major of Miraucourt · Angel Pavement Wonder Hero · Albert Goes Through · They Walk in the City

PLAYS

Dangerous Corner · Eden End · Cornelius · The Roundabout · Laburnum Grove

ESSAYS, ETC.

English Journey · Four in Hand · Brief Diversions · Papers from Lilliput I for One · Talking · Open House · Too Many People · Apes and Angels The Balconinny · Self-selected Essays

CRITICISM

Figures in Modern Literature · The English Comic Characters · Meredith (English Men of Letters) · Peacock (English Men of Letters) · The English Novel · Humour (English Heritage Series)

HARPER & BROTHERS PUBLISHERS

NEW YORK AND LONDON

Established 1817

J. B. Priestley

MIDNIGHT ON THE DESERT

BEING

AN EXCURSION INTO AUTOBIOGRAPHY

DURING A WINTER IN AMERICA

1935-36

HARPER & BROTHERS PUBLISHERS

NEW YORK AND LONDON

1937

To
Edward and Natalie Davison
and old friendship

MIDNIGHT ON THE DESERT

Chapter One

LET me begin with what I can remember quite clearly.
It was at the end of my stay on the ranch in Arizona,
last winter. We were not leaving America yet, but we
were leaving this ranch very soon, and I had things to
do. There was the usual accumulated litter of letters
and odd papers to be gone through, and most of it destroyed. But that was not all. I had decided during
the evening to burn certain chapters, many thousands of
words, of the book I had been writing. I felt I must do
this at once, for I am not a resolute man and do not
trust myself. (But I wish I knew which I really am,
the one who distrusts or the one who is distrusted.
There's the problem.) Yes, thousands and thousands of
words would have to go, along with the rubbish; good
words, all arranged to make sound sense, and with a
cash value in the market, and representing, too, something more than money—time, precious and priceless
time, of which, they say, only so much is allotted to each
of us. I dare not wait for morning. Midnight was the
hour for such a deed.

I left the patio, where we were housed, for the little
hut that was my working-place. I remember a particu-

larly fine glitter of stars, with no moon, and with the desert hills so much starless indigo at the base of the sky. A freight-train was clanking down the valley. It gave that long, dissonant, mournful cry of American trains, that sound which seems to light up for a second the immense distances and loneliness of that country. I had to do some lighting up myself, with a torch, in order to pick my way past prickly pear and cholla and cat-claw and other hooking and spiny growths, vindictive by day and devilish so late at night. The hut was in a little thicket. The sand between the curled dead leaves glittered in the light of my torch; and that would be the specks of fools' gold, with which all these dry river beds and their banks are gilded. It looks much prettier than real gold. Some day perhaps it will be worth quite as much as real gold.

An enormous silence had followed the train; an ironical silence, like that which comes at the end of some noisy epoch. They kept early hours at the ranch, except when there was a dance at *El Recreo*; and there was nobody stirring anywhere; and not a sound even from the coyotes. In the silence, slowly picking my way, I thought about this Arizona country. The New World! It seemed to me the oldest country I had ever seen, the real antique land, first cousin to the moon. Brown, bony, sapless, like an old man's hand. We called it new because it was not thick with history, not a museum and guidebook place. Man had been here such a little time that his arrival had not yet been acknowledged. He was still some season's trifling accident, like a sudden abundance of coyotes or cottontails. The giant saguaro cactus, standing like a sentinel on every knoll, was not on the lookout for us, had not heard of us yet, still waited for trampling dinosaurs. There is no history here because history is too recent. This country is geology by day and astronomy at night. It offers a broad view of what is happening generally in the solar system, with no particular reference to Man. But it has a magnificent routine. The early mornings, in winter, are cold, very fresh and pure. Then, under the burning noons, the red cardinals and the blue-birds flash among the cottonwoods, as if nature had turned outrageously symbolic. The afternoons are simply so much sunlight and aromatic air. But at sunset the land throws up pink summits and saw-toothed ridges of amethyst, and there are miracles of fire in the sky. Night uncovers two million more stars than you have ever seen before; and the planets are not points, but globes. As I reached the door of my hut and switched off my torch, I looked up and noticed yet once again, with a shrinking sense of unfamiliarity, how all the constellations had been monstrously misplaced. I was far from home.

I was not homesick. That is bad, but there is an easy cure for it, if you have the freedom, the money, the passport. You go back to your own place, and all is well. But I was beginning to feel homeless, not homesick.

I had spent all the autumn and the winter in America, and not as a lonely traveler, whose home life is going on somewhere else, but mostly with my family. Thus I seemed to have detached myself from England. This was quite involuntary; it just happened. The island no longer appeared to be the center of the universe. The newspapers that came to me regularly from England now seemed to me as full of quaint fusses and snobberies as they must do to an American reader. Yet I had not had time to throw out any roots in America. Its life, so nervous and strident, so strange a mixture of kindness and cruelty, was still unfamiliar. I was not part of the scene there. Nothing that happened really came home to me. I was deeply interested, but it was all none of my business. I read their newspapers every morning —and they were black with crises—but none of their news was *my* news. I was temporarily a man without a country and a background. Not much harm in that— perhaps if the whole lot of us suddenly found ourselves without countries and backgrounds, there might be much good—but the sensation was new to me and I felt curiously withdrawn, into a dreamy emptiness. Perhaps it made for egoism. We shall see.

The two naked electric bulbs in my hut sharply illuminated its tiny interior, no more than twelve feet by ten of unpainted boards, with many a knothole in them, now velvety with night. There were the rough shelves with their litter of books, tins of tobacco, pipes, and letters I had never answered; the two small tables, one for my typewriter, the other for odds and ends; the straight little chair, too small in the seat, I used when typing, and the armchair with its little square of red and black Indian rug; and the two other Indian rugs on the floor, the woven waste-paper basket, the box of firewood, and the small tin stove, only waiting for a match to be thrown in to shake and roar and be red-hot. Yes, and waiting for anything else I might give it, such as a folder or two of typescript. Seeing everything in there so clearly, all those familiar things of my working day, I felt apologetic. I had come to destroy, not to create; though such destruction might be a better kind of creation.

This hut was a witness to the admirable spirit of Western America, and perhaps of all these states. When I had first stayed on the ranch, the winter before, I had found it hard to work in my bedroom in the patio, where people were always moving about and calling to one another. What I needed was a little place of my own to work in, well away from the main ranch buildings. So as soon as I came back, for a longer stay, up went this shack, and within a day or two it had its book-shelves, stove, and electric light. Nothing very wonderful about all this. It was easily erected, and of course I paid for it. But I feel that in any European country there would have been endless palavers and fusses, whole crops of difficulties raised, before one would have had

[5]

a brand-new place to work in; if indeed one would have persisted in the face of a mountain of objections. Here, in the Far West, it was done so casually and quickly. "You bet!" they cried, and went ahead. Perhaps it is sheer space that makes the difference. What seems obvious and easy in the vast crystalline spaces of Arizona may well appear a tricky enterprise in shuttered Europe. This shack was built on the very edge of a river I have never yet seen, the Hassayampa, which only appears— as a sudden yellow flood—towards the end of summer. If you drink its waters, they say, you are forever afterwards incapable of telling the truth. But the winter visitor does not even see them. This had been a good place to work in. I ask for nothing better. Sometimes in the mornings, before the sun commanded the scene, it had been rather cold and cheerless; and often later in the mornings and during the blazing afternoons, it had been too warm, for there was only one layer of thin boards between me and the weather. But it had been my own place, and quiet, except for an occasional bird that would come to the window, knock with its beak, and stare at me as if we were meeting in Eden. The little hut had served me well.

I had spent most of my time in there, writing a novel about London. With the door and the two windows wide open; a thin curtain drawn to dull the bright shaft of sunlight; wearing nothing but a shirt, old flannel trousers, and slippers, I would sit in a sweet cloud of Amer-

ican tobacco smoke, peer through it at my script, and
tap-tap away at my account of life in the rain and fog
of London streets. There in the middle of my hut, with
Arizona glittering around it for hundreds of miles, was
a tiny dark London, into which I popped every morning
about ten. When people tell you how lucky you are to
be a professional writer, they enumerate advantages
that you know very well are things not worth having;
but they never mention this genuine bit of luck, that
you can sit in Arizona and build for yourself a London
that has just the people, streets, houses, and weather you
need, and can then, months afterwards, sit in Highgate
on a dark wet Monday morning and conjure for yourself the bright illimitable spaces of the Arizona desert.
True, other people can do this, but they must do it on
their own time, for their own amusement; they are not
at liberty to call it work. And it is a dark wet Monday
morning this morning, and I am sitting in Highgate—
working.

When I had gone out there I had meant to spend the
winter writing a novel, but I had had only the vaguest
notion of the form it would take, and so I had not a
single note. I had to remember and invent the London
of my story. Since then, these chapters have been described by reviewers as so many pieces of "brilliant
reporting." They were not intending to be very complimentary: the inference was that reporting was my level.
They may well be right when they hint that the higher,

grander, subtler forms of imaginative writing are quite beyond me; I have never made any great claims myself for my fiction, beyond protesting once or twice that there might be a little more in it than met the top-speed reviewer's eye, and that because I wrote one jolly, hearty, popular novel it does not follow that everything I have written since is exactly the same. But they use words very loosely. To report is to narrate, describe, and repeat as an eye-witness. The reporter is the man on the spot, or he is nothing. Now anyone less on the spot, less of an eye-witness of what he was describing, than myself in that hut can hardly be imagined. A man in Arizona who attempts to describe, with some wealth of detail, what it feels like to be a waitress or a parlor-maid in London, using not one single note, may be a good, bad, or indifferent novelist, but he will certainly not be much of a reporter. He has removed himself far from the scene; he has not prepared himself to describe it; and only by a fairly violent use of his imagination can he identify himself with characters so entirely different from himself. If this is reporting, then I no longer understand the English language.

For truth's sake, and not from any desire to appear a dashing figure of genius, I now put it on record that I would have made a wretched reporter. I have not the energy, the conscience, the trained observation, to report well. I am not sufficiently extraverted. How oddly we are estimated! How fantastic the monsters in public processions, like those in French carnivals, that are carried above our names! Time after time I have seen myself described as an astute, supremely observant, hard fellow, shrewd and pugnacious, smashing his way into best-seller lists. Intelligent people no longer expect to find all Irishmen imaginative and combative, all Scots dour and grasping and given to theological argument. Yet these same people will easily assume that a Yorkshireman must necessarily be shrewd and hard, and that if he goes into authorship, it must be in the same spirit in which a bluff West Riding gambler sets about cornering the Australian wool market.

All this seems to me so ludicrously false that I cannot be angry about it. I have as much self-knowledge as the next man, and probably more than most, and I am ready to declare under oath that I am not very astute nor very observant, am inclined to be timid, irresolute, melancholy, am easily influenced and frequently humbugged, and have neither the enterprise nor the determination to be a hard careerist. I take no thought whatever about a career, make no plans far ahead, but do whatever I want to do, with no reference to its possible dignity or lack of it. I have a restless nature, am easily bored, and so I flit from one kind of work to another, partly sustained by a very genuine interest in the technical problems of all forms of writing. I have always wanted vaguely to be an all-round man of letters on the eighteenth-century plan, which allowed or commanded a man to write essay or poem, novel or play, just as he pleased. This is good fun, but it may not be good business. If you want to play for safety, keeping the career on a steady course, you will do the same thing over and over again—painting two cows in a field, two cows in a field—until at last they write, for the school books, "Nor can we omit a consideration of the leader of the two-cows-in-a-field group . . ." And there you are in your pigeonhole, and not unlike a stuffed pigeon.

It was cold in the hut, so late at night, and now I put a match to the stove, which immediately began roaring and shaking, as it always does in this arid country. Fire needs no coaxing here. It is as if fire were always waiting to be unleashed; just as, in southern California, electricity is always waiting to spark, so that if you walk over a new carpet there, the next thing you touch gives you an electric shock. But everywhere in America, one feels, vast elemental forces may be released from a temporary bondage at one single touch. You may be overwhelmed by them at any moment. Fire and flood, drought and blizzard, hurricane and earthquake, wait in the wings, ready to play their parts in horrible transformation scenes. Nature is not on man's side there. He has only a dubious leasehold.

Now the stove was shaking and glaring, its red eye fixed on my manuscript. Suppose I popped the whole lot in. They were mine to do what I liked with, these hundreds of sheets of typescript, and yet what a fuss there would be! I thought of the three separate firms of publishers, all waiting with that air of modest expectation which is part of their charm, all with spring and autumn lists almost ready for the printer, all with travelers promising wonders to the booksellers, all with directors' meetings and shareholders' meetings and statements to the bank and financial commitments and complications beyond my understanding. Thinking of them, I began wondering whether there was not something false, perhaps ultimately fatal, in this combination of authorship, a tricky and moody activity, with big business, which demands safely standardized products. Perhaps authors were happier when they collected what they could from a patron or did a modest deal with a bookseller. But then I remembered certain facts in the history of literature, and told myself not to be an ass. For there I was, having comfortably conveyed myself and my family halfway around the world, whereas in other times I might have been shivering in a garret, wondering how to find another pair of boots for the children. But even so, it did not seem very healthy to feel that at the other end of the silken cord that runs from your desk are City directors and accountants and rows of debenture-holders, all wondering what the devil you are doing. Very soon the debenture-holders might ask authors to appear before them, to give an account of themselves, explain what it is they are doing, and how many hours a day they are working. Though even then the authors would win. Not even Moscow, not even Hollywood, has ever quite succeeded in putting and keeping authors in their proper places. But the direct method may be less effective than the indirect, the influence of big business in publishing, the author's knowledge that at the other end are accountants and balance sheets waiting.

And I remembered that during my short writing life there had been sad changes in publishing. In the old days a good publisher cast about for authors, solid professional writers, he could believe in, and was then prepared to spend years building up a public for those authors. Now there is a bargain-basement atmosphere about publishing. What are wanted are not growing reputations and sound lists, but snap successes, the Book of the Month, the Smash Hit of the Season. An unemployed governess reveals her subconscious. A taxi-driver's first and last novel. The autobiography of a wholesale grocer suffering from acute melancholia. The expelled schoolgirl's memoirs. And so forth. Where the old publisher had a training-stable, the new one sits down and picks winners. Last week he published another work of astounding genius, and next week he will have forgotten its title.

A month's work was waiting to be destroyed. It could wait a little longer. I was not sleepy. I cut down the glare of the stove, settled in the larger chair, and lit a pipe. The desert was quiet. The coyotes were not howling yet. I was my own howling coyote. Outwardly a comfortable-looking man in an armchair, smoking a pipe, I was inside a half-starved little coyote, out there on the dark desert, howling to the stars. That was my state of mind: a black mood, though a trifle luxurious in its blackness, a velvety blackness, like the trappings at a rich man's funeral. Then, compelled to make some movement, my mind traveled slowly back through the winter, to the autumn before, to the September morning when I had arrived in New York.

Chapter Two

IT DID not begin well. I am one of those people who usually begin a long journey in the liveliest spirits. This is not because I am one of your born travelers. I lack the courage and resourcefulness. I suspect I am a born escaper. I am not steady enough, brave enough, to plant my standard on a hillock and cry, "Here I stay!" The folk who are the salt of the earth are those who settle in one place, whether town or country, and make it their own, finally leaving it much better than they found it. I have often wished I was one of them. But behind me there must be a long line of wandering artisans, mountebanks, and other rubbishy unstable people, who have left me a legacy of restlessness and irresponsibility. It will be all right, I think, if I move on. So I welcome a good long journey. But my traveling has not the right resolute quality, which probably belongs to the traveling of people who have deep roots at home; behind its rather imposing façade—for I can play the easy knowing traveler with some cunning—is uneasiness, the desire to shuffle, dodge, escape; and so I am not happy on my travels and get little out of them. The beginning, however, is the glorious moment of escape, and as a rule nobody enjoys it more than I do. But this time, something was wrong.

I traveled alone, because I was going out to New York to do a play, and my family were not sailing until the end of the month and were then going all the way to the Pacific Coast by sea, through the Panama Canal. But a very good friend of mine, due to make his first appearance on the American stage, was sailing by the same boat. She was the *Aquitania*, one of the pleasantest of the big liners, a comfortable, friendly, family-party sort of boat. And there were some amusing people on board. Nothing was wrong with what Americans call "the set-up." Yet everything was wrong. I felt depressed, perhaps by the state of the world, perhaps by the state of my liver, when we left Southampton; and all the cocktails and caviare, deck tennis and table tennis, bridge and poker, talking pictures and talking passengers, provided by the Cunard White Star Company could not prevent my sinking into a deeper despondency. The sea may have had something to do with it. Elevators and glass-inclosed decks and garden lounges and steel shopping streets—and there is something almost heroic in the spectacular urban idiocies of these ships—cannot make you forget the presence of this huge element, at once so menacing and melancholy.

During the last ten years, I had crossed over fifty thousand miles of ocean, and I had come to know something about it. The sea does not make me sick: it makes me rather afraid and very sad. After that first delicious morning out, in a world newly-washed and sprinkled with salt, an unutterable sadness begins to steal into the heart of things. I look down at the changing patterns of foam in despair. Even the blue days and long soft nights of the Pacific do not comfort me. Some writers I know can go to sea to work; but I cannot work properly there, can hardly think: at the best I am in a sleepy haze, and at the worst I am sunk into the profoundest melancholy.

And this was not the Pacific, but the North Atlantic, one of the unfriendliest of seas; and nearly all the way across the sky was like a dishcloth and the water like so many shifting mounds of slate. And the news that the world poured into the ship, which had the worst items neatly printed and circulated, came from Abyssinia and Italy, Geneva and London, and was bad. And my friend the actor and I wandered about these seesawing steel streets, drank too many whiskies, and asked one another why we were not enjoying ourselves. There awoke then a sense of oncoming disaster, impending doom, that has never quite left me since. The ship plunged steadily towards New York, but the shadow went with us.

But it lifted for our arrival. The morning that saw us into the Hudson was as clear and clean as a new penny. The river sparkled, the early autumn air was as good as an apple, and the melancholy of the sea was forgotten. The city that towered from the waterfront seemed more beautiful than ever, still more incredible, the only city in the world. I could look at it entranced, at my ease, because this time the reporters and photographers who had boarded us off Quarantine did not regard me as their special prey. I was no longer front-page stuff, thank Heaven! It was a pity I ever had been. The only visitor to any country who should be handled as if he were first-rate news is the man who comes on a definite mission of social importance, for he has something to say and welcomes the coöperation of the Press. But what can the other visitors—authors and film stars and the like—say to the reporters? What questions worth answering can the reporters ask them? It is all very fatuous. We in England give a hoot of derision when yet another Hollywood star tells us she thinks our police are wonderful. The American public must have been exasperated for years now by the printed comments, real or imaginary, of new arrivals in New York. It is the visitor who has not yet seen America, who is still straining his eyes to catch a glimpse of it through the morning mists of the Hudson River, who is asked what he thinks of America. And he will be lucky if he is not also asked what he thinks of American women, as if American women were specimens of some rare creature kept in a few cages here and there in these States. A harmless man of letters, arriving for the first time in a great country, is bewildered when it sends its representatives to inquire what he thinks of all its wives and sisters and daughters. He comes to the conclusion that it must be a joke. The reporters themselves, who are no fools, know that it is all a joke. Their talk among themselves about visiting celebrities must be very rich. Unfortunately, a great many newspaper-readers, on both sides of the Atlantic, take these fatuous interviews quite seriously. Some very rum people read newspapers.

Now and again, of course, it may get beyond a joke. The last time I had landed in America, I had traveled in a ship that stayed a few hours at Boston, to discharge cargo, and while she was there a young man from a news syndicate came to interview me. I was extremely brief and guarded, merely giving him a few facts, such as that I had recently done some film work and was now on my way to Arizona for a short holiday. A few hours later there went out to the entire Press of the United States the following item:

J. B. Priestly, English novelist, playwright and critic, arrived from England today, en route to New York aboard the *Britannic* with the observation that "America has a general case of indigestion" and Boston was an "over-rated" city of "mock culture."

His discourse left little doubt that he didn't think so much of New York, either. He was convinced, he said, that London had stolen from New York the right to be known as the dramatic capital of the civilized world.

The vigorous, forty-year-old Englishman remained on board the vessel during its stay here. He concluded his description of Boston by saying that, like the rest of the United States, "it is in a bad way with afflictions of silly, childish movies, bad plays, and cheap novels." Priestly, who at present is writing sequences in a motion-picture play, is on his way to Arizona, with Mrs. Priestly, to obtain "local color."

"Bah" and "puerile" were his answers to questions regarding American movies. American people, he asserted, eat too many sweet things and have "a national case of indigestion." He added that "sometimes I think it's caused by the movies over here."

It is a fact that not one single remark attributed to me in the above report ever passed my lips during this interview. And it does not need a Sherlock Holmes to discover from the report itself the writer's glaring inaccuracy. To begin with, he cannot spell my name properly, and he has no excuse, for while there are thousands of Priestleys in the world, I have yet to meet a single Priestly. That, however, is a small error. Consider the phrases within quotation marks, which are supposed to be my exact words. The locution is all wrong; no English writer would talk like that; but a careless young American reporter, returning to his office to invent something lively for me to say, might very well write like that. Then again, he makes me "conclude" my description of Boston by saying "it is in a bad way with afflictions" of this and that; but if I had given him a description of Boston, of which this sentence was the mere conclusion, why hadn't he reported the

[19]

whole description, for clearly, on his own showing, my opinion of Boston was of some interest to his readers? Now he says himself that I stayed aboard the ship and therefore did not visit Boston on this occasion. But if I could describe the city—and to a reporter who had just come from it—then I must have visited it on some previous occasion. As he was a Boston reporter, you would think he would have told his readers when it was I had visited Boston. He did not tell them because he knew very well I had never been to Boston, and he knew that because I told him so when I refused to pass any judgment on the character of that city. I am capable of generalizing very wildly about places I have stayed in, even if only for a few days, but I never pass severe judgments on cities I have never set foot in, and if ever I did break this rule, the last person I should choose as a confidant would be a reporter from that particular city. And I have never in this life answered anybody's question by replying "Bah!" I am not a member of the Bah association. But I can promise that young reporter that if ever he catches me again, the only reply he can hope to get to any question to me is Bah, Bah, and a thousand times Bah.

When I arrived in New York and promptly denied having talked such balderdash, I was treated with great courtesy by the head of this news syndicate, who apologized for such a flagrant misrepresentation and ordered the interview to be withdrawn at once. I am afraid, however, that by that time the mischief was done. I am still occasionally referred to as the English writer who does not like America. This is ironical because I happen to be one of the very few English writers who frequently visit America, not because of any lecture tour or film contract, but for its own sake. I have a sincere and deep interest in the American scene. I have been critical of American life, but only as I have been critical of any life I have ever known, because such is my nature; but I have never been supercilious and patronizing. I could be happy working for people so hearty, plain-spoken, democratic, for I feel nearer to them than I do to certain more elaborate types of English. And as I have talked and listened to American citizens of all kinds from Providence, Rhode Island, to San Diego, California, I am not writing in ignorance. And this very autumn I had brought nine persons, including all my children, from London to the Far West, and had kept them there for half a year at very substantial charges to myself. This does not suggest much dislike of the country.

As I looked down on the customs shed and the little group of friends waiting for me there (and how much precious time New Yorkers must waste seeing their friends arrive or depart, and all without a murmur!) I told myself severely that for once I must take New York quietly, as just another city. I had some work to do—to produce my play—and I must do that work as

calmly as if I were at home in London. (I overlooked
the fact that it is quite impossible for me to produce a
play calmly anywhere; for that mad old witch, the
Theater, tolerates no calmness.) I must not let this city
steal my wits. But even then I could feel the mounting
excitement. It would happen all over again. I would
arrive, and for a day or two be a man reeling in an
enchantment. All other cities would seem in retrospect
like mere huddles of mud huts. Here, once more, would
be Babylon and Nineveh in steel and concrete, the island
of shining towers, all the urban poetry of our time. All
kinds of nonsense might be going on inside Radio City,
but the buildings themselves would soar above my criticism. I would hurry down these canyons and gulfs they
call avenues, cry out as one magnificent vista of towers
crowns another, hold my breath at nightfall to see the
glittering palaces in the sky, and wonder how I can ever
again endure the gloomy and stunted London.

And then, if I stayed on—and this was to be my
longest stay in New York, if the play were to be produced—three things would happen, all bad. First, I
would suffer much physical discomfort, would find myself hotter or colder, drier in the mouth, thicker in the
head, than I am anywhere else. Secondly, I would find
it impossible to sleep more than two or three hours at
a time; and the quietest apartment, the most cautious
dinner or supper, the most artful preparations for sleep,
would make no difference. Oh!—those nights of wake-

fulness, with the mind racing away, noisily, uselessly, like the accelerated engine of a stationary motor. There is to me still some mystery about this sleeplessness of mine in New York. The air, the change of habit, the wining and dining, will explain something, but not all of it. There is a deep inner excitement, like that of a famished lover waiting for his mistress, that I cannot account for—not when it outlasts the mere novelty of arrival and goes on week after week—but I know that it crackles and burns at the heart of this strange insomnia. Possibly the third bad thing follows naturally from this, for a man who is weeks behind with his sleep is in no normal state of mind; but I knew I would be visited, after the first enchantment of landing there had vanished, by a growing feeling of spiritual desolation.

I would begin to feel empty inside. It would be impossible for me to sit still and be quiet. I must go somewhere, eat and drink with a crowd, see a show, make a noise. Time must not merely be killed, but savagely murdered in public. In this mood, which has never missed me yet in New York, I feel a strange apprehension, unknown to me in any other place. The city assumes a queer menacing aspect, not only to me, I feel, but to all the people I know there. I begin to fancy that perhaps it is waiting for some other kind of people—chromium-plated giants without dreams or tenderness—to come along and claim it. Most capital cities are an obvious expression of their communities. London is English life in brick, chimney-pots, old squares, smoke, and mist. There is all French life somewhere in Paris. But when Americans say that New York does not represent America, they are leaving much unsaid. It is true that you cannot meet representative Americans in New York as you can meet representative Britons in London or the gallery of leading French types in Paris. But that is not all, only the beginning.

I feel that New York represents something, but not anything clearly known to me. It is rather like looking at another planet. The architectural values of the city cannot be related to our ordinary human values, and so seem queer, disturbing. I have had it explained to me many a time exactly what economic forces were at work in Manhattan to create this towering city, and how a simple geography and geology have played their part in its structure. But I am not convinced, not satisfied. I know a man in New York, a very intelligent man who has spent his life there, who can produce a very amusing burlesque of the kind of literary rhapsody on the city that visitors like myself never fail to create, who roars with laughter at all this fancifulness as he points out that a few simple facts completely explain New York. The trouble is, though, that he himself seems almost equally strange to me; I have watched him drink half the night and never seem gayer or sadder; I am always puzzled by his way of life, his values; so nothing he says can throw a light on the mystery of his city. My deep uneasiness remains, grows, even accompanying me into the houses of friends there, calm, smiling, hospitable friends. Outside those houses, it begins to take on a nightmare quality. I feel like a midget character moving in an early scene of some immense tragedy, as if I had had a glimpse in some dream, years ago, of the final desolation of this city, of seabirds mewing and nesting in these ruined avenues. Familiar figures of the streets begin to move in some dance of death. That barker outside the Broadway burlesque show, whose voice has almost rusted away from inviting you day and night to step inside and see the girls, now seems a sad demon croaking in hell. The traffic's din sounds like the drums in the March to the Gallows of a *Symphonie Fantastique* infinitely greater, wilder, more despairing than Berlioz'.

Yes, this is all very fanciful, of course, the literary mind playing with images; yet the mood behind it, that feeling of spiritual desolation, that deepening despair, are real enough. And nowhere else in America do I catch a glimpse of this Doomsday Eve. Only New York does that to me. Too much excitement and not enough sleep will account for a good deal, but will they account for everything? Or has something been seen, some faint glimmer of writing on one of these walls, some echo of the voice that was suddenly heard, pronouncing judgment, at Babel?

The New York I landed in this time could think of

nothing but the Baer-Louis fight, which was taking place that very evening. The restaurant where I dined with some friends had installed enormous loud speakers, to give us the broadcast commentary on the fight. Once it began, the waiters forgot us, and we forgot the food on our tables. But I found it extremely difficult to understand what was happening in the ring. Instead of giving us a clear technical account of the fight, as one of the calm, superior, irritating but efficient, B.B.C. men would have done, this American commentator shouted bad rhetoric at us—"Say, it's terrific—brown thunderbolts, black lightning!" and so forth—and communicated nothing but his frenzied excitement, of which we stood in no need. He turned himself into an extension of our nerves instead of our eyes. He deafened and exhausted us, but told us little or nothing.

Now what saves a big prize fight from being a mere exhibition of bestiality is the fact that the two men engaged in it are not only highly-trained, but are also highly-skilled. There is technique, a bit of science and a bit of art, in the business. But this commentator, who apparently was an expert and knew what was expected of him, so contrived his broadcast that we never got a glimpse of technique: only the unhealthy nervous excitement came through, the bestial drama. And I felt once more that the American crowd is often curiously hysterical, far removed from the cool Yankee of tradition. There is, too, a disturbing suggestion of cruelty in this crowd hysteria. The average American citizen, acting quietly on his own, is long-suffering and kind and impulsively generous. But turn him into a crowd, a public, and he becomes one of an oddly savage and intolerant mob, lacking loyalty and affection, eager to trample on its idols of yesterday, ready to destroy ruthlessly, almost sadistically. Why, I do not know. Something in the electric air, perhaps; the mixture of races; the influence of the vast plains and their intemperate seasons; the reaction from monotonous little jobs of work; the strain and savage competition of business life —all these may contribute. But there it is, and I met it full-face on this first evening of my return to New York.

After too much boasting and clowning, Baer lost rather too easily; and never have I heard a man so savagely dismissed. He might have been a statesman they had trusted for years and who had sold millions of them into slavery. Enough energy and indignation went into the dismissal of this unhappy prize-fighter to have cleaned up the politics of the whole country. Whatever else he made, he made a magnificent red herring. Off they went, swarming and howling, leaving a comparative few, referred to as fanatics and Reds, still pointing to the trail that led to political corruption and cynical exploitation. But I am overshooting my own mark.

I had already had three plays of mine produced in New York, unseen by me, and each time I had been told that they had not been done properly and that I ought to have seen to them myself. So this time I proposed to supervise the production, if only because this particular play, "Eden End," was my favorite. It was not simply that it was my best play—it still remains that—but that also I had for it a special tenderness, like that which some parents feel for a certain child. I had thought about the people in it for years, had lived with them, so when the time came to write it, I went into the country in the summer of 1934, and after a week or two of happy absorption, that utterly self-forgetful creative zest which more than pays for all the sick vanity and vexation of an author's life, I began and finished all its three acts. Its production in London had been a success; not a "smash hit," because it was not that kind of play; but it had been generously praised, in and out of print, by people whose opinion I valued, and it had run at a profit for over a hundred and fifty performances. Afterwards, all the repertory and Little Theater companies in the country had given performances of it. A lot of people did not like it at all, but the people who did like it found something more than an evening's entertainment in it, were caught and held by the life that I had imagined, were moved as I had been moved; and no writer can reasonably ask more than that.

This, then, was the piece, very near and dear to me, that I had come to New York to produce. I had high hopes of it, partly because I understood that there was more demand for intelligence and sincerity in the Theater in New York than in London, and also because a number of Americans connected with the Theater had seen it in London and had been enthusiastic about it. On the other hand, I was a stranger on Broadway and this was not an easy play to do, and so I knew that I was in for trouble. But, then, no man who wanted to avoid trouble would ever have anything to do with the Theater.

Why had I suddenly changed course and gone from miscellaneous writing and novels into the Theater? Sitting there in that hut in Arizona, feeling very much alone in the sleeping desert, I put this question very seriously to myself and did my best to find an honest answer. We have often been told by dramatists, who like us to think they are masters of a Mystery, that novelists envy them their noisier and more glittering successes. But I knew at once this would not do. The Theater, for all its noise and glitter, is a tiny world. Most of the people who work in it do not realize how small it is because they never take the risk of stepping outside it. But the writer of books, whose post may bring him letters from the ends of the earth, knows what a miniature world the dramatist lives in. He knows, too, that he has only to begin writing for the Theater to vanish completely from the minds of thousands of his readers, who may not be at the ends of the earth, but actually living within sight of the theaters where he is working. He also knows that once a book is in print, sooner or later it will find a way to its readers, whereas a play is at the mercy of circumstance, the chance of finding the proper players, the right theater. A dramatist always is in the position of a novelist who, on completing his book, finds that now he has to go around looking for a likely compositor and printer, a paper merchant to be flattered into friendliness, a bookbinder caught in the right mood, booksellers that have to be treated like hysterical babies. The novelist who has written his novel has finished. The dramatist who has finished his play has hardly begun; he is still in fair possession of his nervous energy and self-esteem; but by the time the dramatic critics, looking sulky, have sunk into their seats for the first night, he will be a wreck, a shadow. So much was known to me before I made a move towards the Theater. I have my illusions, but they are not of this kind. So much for the noise and the glitter.

Nor was it money, though the very successful dramatist can make more than even the most successful novelist. But the dramatist who is not extremely lucky can have years of dead loss, impossible to the novelist who has good health and a firm of publishers behind him. Unlike readers of books, the theatrical public has no loyalty to its authors, only to its actors; and Shakespeare could return from the grave next week and have a flop. As a dramatist, you can burn up months of your life, and have no return for them but charred nerves. I have met a few disappointed and permanently soured novelists and essayists, but I know far more disappointed and permanently soured dramatists. They have years and years of work hopelessly awaiting production. I have yet to meet a novelist with any name who had cupboards filled with unpublished stories. And long before I penciled in my first cast, I knew all this.

What then was the compulsion, the force that hurled me towards these barriers? It was the ancient witchery of the work itself, the eternal fascination of the Theater. And by the Theater I do not mean Shaftesbury Avenue and Broadway, for I am not too fond of the metropolitan theatrical world, with its smart hangers-on, its mysterious financial gentlemen, its supper-room exhibitionists, its "You were marvelous, darling" nonsense. No, I mean the essential Theater, wherever it may be. Indeed, I believe I should be happiest working with some stock company in an unfashionable town, if the actors were reasonably good and the audience not too hopelessly dull. The Theater seems more glamorous to me when it suddenly pops up in the side street of some dreary industrial town than it does when there are rows of it, blazing with neon signs, in one of the capitals. My heart leaps up when I behold the Theatre Royal, Coketown.

After years of working alone, as the writer of books must do, there is a deep satisfaction—no matter how much wrangling there may be—in working with other people, as the dramatist does. Even now I know a man

[31]

may tire of it, may return in relief to his study. But even the temporary loyalties and team work of the Theater of today, with its too flimsy organization, are a welcome break. That, however, does not explain the fascination. I have to go back to my teens to find the real explanation. As a youth I was a passionate play-goer, and for some time was determined to go on the stage myself. (A good comic actor was lost in me, or almost lost.) Then other ambitions came, sweeping me away from the Theater, through poetry and journalism, the barren interlude of the war, then afterwards through criticism, essays, and fiction; but the movement was circular, and after twenty years or so I found myself thinking hard about the Theater again; but this time, being a professional writer, as a dramatist. And I did not hesitate to turn manager for myself, too, learning a good deal in the rather grim process. The witchery still remained; but now it was more than an unreasoning adulation of histrionics. I came to see that the Theater, though much of its appeal may be childish, is an institution that cannot be safely despised even by the philosopher. It is indeed one of the few common meeting-places of the child and the wise adult. It is rich in symbols.

The actor himself is such a clearly symbolic figure that I always find it hard to resist the temptation to write about him. His sharply-colored, ironic life is a parody of all our lives. There is more in "All the world's a stage" than first meets the eye. Where there is self-consciousness, there—you may say—the Theater has set up its platform and curtains. We all play character parts, day and night. We are haunted by a feeling that we are acting in a gigantic masque. It is significant that in the ancient world the Theater was a religious institution. I am not sure that the link between Religion and the Theater has been broken forever. One of our few contemporary prophets, George Bernard Shaw, has chosen to work in the Theater. Now, some of the most earnest of our young poets are obviously being attracted towards it. Perhaps we may have a new serious Theater that will be the servant of a religion that has not yet taken shape. To many of our contemporaries Communism is a substitute for religion, and, for all its austerity, Communism seems to turn instinctively towards the Theater.

With intelligence and sincere emotion behind it, a theatrical production, that mimic piece of life colored and contrived to the wink of an eyelash, is a very rich, four-dimensional kind of creation, a tiny epitome of the universal drama of creation. Thus we could enlarge the meaning of Hamlet's description of the players as "the abstracts and brief chronicles of the time." They may paint their faces to take part in a Mystery. And I suspect that it may be some obscure but deep-seated apprehension of this, and not simply the glitter and applause, the possibility of easy fame, the erotic atmosphere, the

[33]

escape through exhibitionism, the whole glamorous bag of tricks, that leads men and women to sacrifice their time, their health, their peace of mind in the service of the Theater. Not Broadway, not Shaftesbury Avenue, but the essential Theater, the place around the corner where they are doing a play tonight.

Guarded flank and rear by agents, melancholy men whose lack of illusion was appalling, I had to form some sort of syndicate to produce the play. This was a wearisome long job, much longer than it would have been in London. There were several good reasons for all the delays. My associates did not seem to trust one another a single step. Then there were strange Oriental problems of "face"—such as, Whose office notepaper shall we use?—that had to be settled. And I discovered that the famous hustle of New York was mythical in these transactions. Everybody gave the impression of being overwhelmed with work; rang bells and barked hastily into batteries of desk telephones; said "Yep" and "Yeh" and "Yah," as if there simply was not time for "Yes"; but the actual business was done in slow motion. They would not talk over the telephone; you had to see them, and they were always to be found almost as inaccessible as Grand Lamas, on the thirtieth story of some building that took you an hour to reach, through the thick porridge tide of New York traffic.

Once you had penetrated into their private offices, they welcomed you as a brother, put you into an easy-chair, and then sent through the cigar smoke at you some twenty or thirty thousand words of autobiography. A prospective historian of the American theatrical and film industries could ask for no better treatment. Unfortunately, I had a play to produce and only so many weeks to do it in. When I ventured to refer, apologetically, to the business in hand, their looks hinted at a breach of manners, making me feel like a man who had suddenly tried to sell his hostess a vacuum cleaner. When they were tired of talking in one place, we went out and looked at empty theaters, of which New York had a surprisingly large number at that time. They were nearly all very neglected and forlorn—though still enchanting—and they served as an excellent start for fresh batches of theatrical memoirs. It was hard going. I felt like a man condemned to walk for days across a colossal wet plowed field.

Meanwhile, a clammy Indian summer had settled on the city. The sunlight seemed to have substance and weight. It poured into Park, Madison, and Fifth Avenues, which I seemed to cross and recross eternally, in cataracts of warm liquid gold. All day my clothes were damp with perspiration. At night my heavy London evening clothes were drenched. And for once profuse sweating did not make for cheerfulness. The mood that had lifted at my landing had come down on me again, darker than ever. The morning papers that come out in the evening, and the evening papers that arrive all morning, were black and dripping with threats of war. The League of Nations, which had seemed to some of us the last chance political mankind had to civilize itself, had now taken the place of the defeated Baer as chief target for ridicule. The other English I met confirmed my gloom.

Nor were my American friends much more cheerful. The obvious signs of distress—the bread lines and apple-sellers—that I had noticed before in New York seemed to be missing now. You could openly buy a drink when you wanted one; and somehow you were often wanting one. There was plenty of organized and expensive gayety at night. The famous dance bands had returned to their supper-rooms. New shows were opening. But people were excited rather than cheerful. They were in the mood for hard, nervous, noisy plays with the maximum of obvious theatricality; machine-gun stuff in drama. They did not want to be quiet, even for a couple of hours. They wanted more excitement on top of their own excitement. Nobody felt secure. They were still wandering in that dark forest that sprang up around them so suddenly in 1929. Roosevelt had let a gleam or two of sunlight into a clearing here and there, but as yet they felt they were not out of the wood. The news that Europe seemed about to commit suicide saddened the thoughtful and did nothing to enliven the rest, beyond the momentary sense of superiority that was given them with every five cents' worth of newsprint. This city of high towers, so radiant in the autumn sunshine, had no peace of mind. It was moving along its time track towards an unknown destination. Nobody had a compass and a chart. The great buildings seemed contemptuously alien to the life out of which they flowered. In the Rainbow Room of Radio City, a warmed and scented mountain summit, where the windows frame all Manhattan and leagues beyond, a peak of human ingenuity, a Babel that has escaped the ancient curse, we gathered at midnight to hear a woman at a piano sing dirty songs. No age but ours could have planted that shining place so securely in the sky. No age but ours would have dreamed of using it as a temple of cheap smut.

Some of the young New York writers, artists, intellectuals, I had been told more than once, were going over to Communism. This time I had a chance of becoming acquainted with some of them and their works. They were not impressive. It is possible to disengage three different types of Communist, although they are not entirely separate. The first is the philosophical, who accepts with grim joy the iron dialectic. Here, he says, is intellectual order in a chaos; and is converted. The second is primarily moved by compassion. Years ago he would have been a Socialist, would have read his Ruskin and Morris. Now he is a Communist, waits for the Golden Age, and is somewhat uneasy when he hears what steps may be necessary to bring it into being. He is eager to explain that Russia is very Russian, that the

[37]

process of "liquidation" is not so bad when you are on the Steppes, just something Russian like vodka and kicking your heels in the air. The third seems possessed by a snarling inferiority. To him Communism is not so much his plan for the world as his revenge on the world. If you do not instantly recognize his merit, that is because you are still squirming under the thumb of the Boss Class. Among the young New York Communists I met several specimens of this class, more indeed than I did of the other two. And I read some examples of "Marxist criticism" of literature that would have sent old Karl Marx himself into a rage.

The best achievement of the Reds that I encountered was the production of Clifford Odets' "Waiting for Lefty," which seemed to shake the theater with a revolutionary fury. I could imagine a popular drama of great power sprouting from such a seed. But a full-sized play of his, "Awake and Sing" that I also saw appeared to me to have been over-praised; it was conventional stuff of no great merit with a few Communist speeches tacked on to it.

The American Communist tends to be noisier and more aggressive than the English Communist of the same type, chiefly, I think, because he feels farther removed from the rest of the political community than the English one does; he alone is wearing the scarlet shirt among all the black coats of the bourgeois; whereas in England he would find himself among shirts of every shade of pink and red.

All those shirts would look almost pale near the autumnal woods of New England. This time, at last, I saw them, in their full glory, as I week-ended with friends up in the Berkshires. I had never seen such woods before. They were a conflagration. Whole counties were on fire. After New York, it was like wandering into a burning Eden. I am a townsman born and bred, and can cheerfully endure miles of streets, but New York is too severely urban for me. I like a glimpse of nature. It is reassuring to know that trees and grass and the birds are still with us. And Central Park does not reassure me. There is something so stony about it that I cannot quite believe in its trees and birds. Nature, I feel, is not really at work there; only the paternal city authorities. All the rest of the New York I had to spend my time in was so much steel and concrete and gasoline vapor. I felt as far removed from the seasons and their pageantry, from dew and wet grass and the autumn berries, as a mummy in a museum. To motor out of it was to discover the real world all over again. Once past the last hot-dog stand, beauty parlor and movie house, the countryside seemed strangely rural, an unkempt farmhouse beauty. But the actual district in which I spent my week-end was not unkempt. It was very gracious, charming, notwithstanding the superb flamboyance of its leaves, all dying like heroes of poetic tragedy.

I was enchanted by the way in which the villages would suddenly appear in the middle of woods. First a delightful wooden house or two, then a main street, with a glimpse of a church, a few last bungalows, and then the woods again. As if a committee of trees had superintended the building of the village. And it was all, from the biggest porch down to the smallest red maple leaf, as deliciously American as Bath and Wells are deliciously English. I might have been back again in the *St. Nicholas* I used to read as a child. The air was very good, clear, and fresh and flavored with the smell of wet leaves; it was invigorating, but had not the almost sinister electric quality of the New York air; it was like honest beer after night-club champagne. Immediately I slept again, instead of merely pretending to myself that I was sleeping as I had been doing in New York; I dropped deeper than plummet ever sounded; and came up next morning ten years younger and twenty years happier. The walk we went after that might have been through one of the happiest poems of Whitman.

One of the attractions of this region is that while you are there you feel obscurely that you are on the edge of a mighty continent—the scale of things is somehow bigger than in England—yet you are not sufficiently far inland to be overwhelmed by the monstrous geography of these states, have no suspicion of hostility in this land-mass, still feel that you can cope with everything. It is not until you travel farther west, leaving the sea, and retreat far behind, that you begin to feel something faintly menacing in the vast landscape. Here, among these burnished hills, I was at peace. It lasted until the final and terrible hour of our drive back to New York on the Sunday night, when a million of us, all cursing and hooting and grinding gears, were trying to cross the Harlem River at the same time; and so we returned to the city the same nervous, depressed creatures who had left it. But there was for me one difference. Now at a touch I could release in my memory the flame and wonder of those woods. I knew at last all that autumn could do.

We had now assembled a fair cast, some of whom had come specially from England, and were hard at it rehearsing them in a draughty shed in Forty-fifth Street that called itself a theater because it had seats in it. (There were cockroaches, too, and they had a trick of appearing just when the leading lady had to be wistful.) In my spare time I had gloomy farewell drinks with various English friends who were leaving for the interior; I went to several "openings" or first nights, which I found as unpleasant in New York as they are in London; I broadcast a talk on England and America and wrote an article or two; I saw the Rodeo in Madison Square Garden and thought it not so blameless as it seemed in the open Western air; I endured half the first performance of the film of "A Midsummer Night's Dream," and then hurriedly left the horror; I lunched and supped at the usual places with friends or new acquaintances, and buzzed around like a bumblebee. I had such a good time that nothing will ever induce me to have one again.

At last our rehearsing was done, and we moved up to New Haven, to see what Yale thought of us, for a night or two. The Connecticut coast, so brown and blue, with a nutty flavor about it, looked a great improvement upon Broadway and Forty-fifth Street. New Haven seemed friendly. Yale took us in and gave us sherry and rye in rooms vaguely reminiscent of the newer colleges in Oxford and Cambridge. The theater was large, badly lit, and appeared to be living not very hopefully on its memories of "Floradora" and "The Witching Hour."

The play opened, not too badly, on the Friday night. On Saturday afternoon, Yale played the Navy at football, and I was taken to the match, the first I had ever seen. I made little of it: a sort of murderous chess, with a grand carnival going on all around it. I took a strong dislike to all the energetic young men who were acting as cheer-leaders: they seemed so self-satisfied in their idiocy. Highly organized cheering belongs to that part of American life and thought which bewilders me, making me feel suddenly that I might as well be among the Chinese. Either cheering is spontaneous or it is nothing. To organize it is to kill it stone-dead. You might as well use an automaton to pat the men on the back as they go into the field.

My play was not the perfect entertainment for a football crowd, but nevertheless it did well that night. We had had a very successful "try-out." Now there was nothing more I could do beyond having a few last words with the director and one or two of the cast. My family would be landing on the west coast in a few days. It was time I was moving west. I should miss the New York opening, but if there was nothing more for me to do, I was only too ready to miss the opening. So on Sunday I climbed into the Twentieth Century Limited, much subdued by the ecclesiastical lighting arrangements of the Grand Central Station.

Just before the train started, the platform, which had been dim and quiet as if it were the crypt of the cathedral that they pretend is the entrance hall, suddenly became crowded and noisy, until it looked as if we were going to have a performance of "Petrushka." But they were all seeing off the little Russian-Jew in the magenta shirt, and they were doing it with cheers, tears, kisses, songs, and dances. Awestruck, I asked who he was, and was told that he had been called from New York, where he had been representing Paramount Films, to Hollywood, to the great beating heart of Paramount Films. And I realized that already California was much nearer, although my train had not yet moved from Grand Central Station. But it carried me away at last, and then another train took me to the high windy platform of Albuquerque, New Mexico.

[43]

It was there, with a cold gritty wind stinging me, that I read the telegrams from New York about the opening of the play. They were as uncomfortable as the wind. Though we actually struggled on for some weeks, I think I knew then that it was all up. And so it turned out. There was not the tiniest glimmer of that enthusiasm for the play which some Americans had shown in London; there was not the tiniest glimmer of anything; the critics were not hostile so much as fantastically incomprehensible, as if they were beings from Mars commenting on my play; I never received one letter about it, not even of abuse; it was as if the whole production had been dropped into the Hudson River: I felt like a man who had quietly arranged a show of etchings in a Home for the Blind. I think I knew all this on that station platform of Albuquerque as I crumpled the Western Union forms and turned my face to the stinging particles of that windy night. So that was that. Come wind, come rack!

Chapter Three

I PUT some more wood in the stove, for these fires die down as suddenly as they flare and blaze, and though the hut was small and the stove had been roaring at it for the last ten minutes, the walls were thin, there were many knot-holes and gaping seams, and the night was cold. The winter had gone, passing as lightly over this desert country as a cloud, and each day was warmer; but the nights were still cold. Nothing broke the silence: no late ranch guests came hooting up the deeply rutted track from Wickenburg; the coyotes were quiet; no other train had passed over the line from Ash Fork to Phœnix. As I settled again in the armchair and lit another pipe, I returned to those trains that had carried me west the autumn before.

Because I could do no more for the play they were taking back into Forty-fifth Street, I tried in the train to dismiss it from my mind and to think exclusively of the novel I proposed to write during the winter. As one grows older and more cunning in one's profession, one learns to escape from the foolish trick of waiting, after a piece of work is done, to see what happens to it when it is offered to the public. A young writer feels that it is hopeless to attempt anything else until the fate of the last novel or play is more or less settled. He walks about with quivering nerve-ends exposed for months. An older hand knows that this won't do. The anxiety, the hope and the fear, are all there, but he tries to bury them deep, and covers the surface of his mind with plans for the next job. So now, out to Chicago and afterwards on "The Chief" as it clanked across Kansas and climbed into New Mexico, I thought about my novel. And it needed some thinking about.

This is a queer time for novelists. I wonder how many readers consider the obstacles we have to face. The time-scheme alone. If we go back only twenty-five years we are in the pre-war period, almost writing historical stuff. Back twenty years and we are plump in the middle of the war, which is impossible to ignore. Do you want another war novel? No, you do not. Fifteen years, then? That means 1920-21, the immediate post-war period; and you know all about that. Even ten years back and we are in the middle of the 'twenties, a not very hopeful setting. The time, then, is the present. Give us, please, you cry, the real world, not some triviality taking place in a pretty-pretty imaginary world, no mere escape stuff. Certainly, madam; certainly, sir. Now what is happening in this real world? The Communists and the Fascists are demonstrating and counter-demonstrating, preparing for a fight; the economic system of our fathers is breaking down;

Europe is bristling with armaments and gigantic intoler-
ances, Asia is stirring out of her ancient dream, America is bewildered and bitter; one kind of civilization is
rapidly vanishing and God-knows-what is taking its
place; some men are marching in column of fours,
shouting slogans, and making ready to kill and be
killed; some men—many of them in exile because their
minds are honest and not without distinction—are arguing in a melancholy circle; other men are lining up in
the hope of finding a little bread, a little work, a little
peace of mind. Here is material enough for a novelist.
But no, no, no, this will not do, you tell us: you want a
novel, a fiction to take you out of yourselves, not a newspaper, a fat pamphlet, a slab of propaganda. After all,
private life goes on; men still fall in love, women fall
out of it; there are entertaining quarrels between the
Smiths and the Robinsons; young men are suddenly
promoted and girls are given fur coats and diamond
bracelets; and there is still plenty of comic stuff about
—oh, uproariously comic stuff. This being so, get on
with your novel, and don't give yourself airs, don't
come the propagandist, the gloomy prophet, over us.

All very fine, but can it be done? If we find contemporary men and women laboriously climbing and bruising themselves against great rocks, and we are told to
show a picture of them, how are we to leave out the
rocks? True, the picture need not be all rocks. But the
rocks must come into it, if we are to be truthful and

sincere. And perhaps the most baffling problem of the modern novelist, who wishes to be a sincere and not insignificant observer and yet believes that there must be charm and entertainment in the art of fiction, is the proportion of rocks to people in the composition. You may be sure too that whatever he decides, he will be blamed. He may succeed in displeasing everybody. Lucky enough in other respects, I have been unlucky in this.

Some years ago, because I had long cherished the plan and was now in the mood to work it out, I wrote a long, comic, *picaresque,* fairy-tale sort of novel, called *The Good Companions.* I am neither prouder nor more ashamed of having written it than I am of having written any of the other books and plays under my name. But it happened to achieve an astonishing popularity. Since then—and this is an exact statement—I do not think I have met or corresponded with five-and-twenty persons who have not blamed me, either for having written this particular novel, or for not having written a lot of other novels just like it. One party denounces me as a hearty, insensitive lowbrow. The other party asks what the devil I mean by turning myself into a gloomy highbrow. If there are more than twenty-five sane folk who have not joined either party, I have not had the luck to meet them. I am condemned—and for a long term, it seems—to offend all round. Merely by publishing anything at all, I must put myself, right and left, in the wrong. Thus I have my private worry waiting for me, even when I have settled the problem set every conscientious novelist of our time.

No wonder, then, my new novel needed some thinking out. I was not bored on those trains.

My immediate task was to find the right setting, the most suitable scheme of action, the best manner of narration, for what seemed to me an attractive and not unworthy idea. This was to take two simple young people, typical specimens of the exploited and helpless class, to bring them together, part them, bring them together again, in the fashion of the oldest and simplest love stories, but to place them and their little romance within a strong framework of social criticism. The two youngsters would be symbolic figures rather than solidly created characters. Much of what happened to them would be symbolic of the special difficulties and dangers of the large class they represented. Like a scarlet thread running through the narrative would be the fairy-tale of young love, as this boy and girl saw it; but the reader's mind would be constantly yanked away from their viewpoint to a wide and critical survey of the social scene. If, for example, they met in a teashop, I would try to convey the wonder and glow of that meeting, but at the same time I would examine the institution of the teashop itself, relating it to a sharp analysis, which would develop with the story, of our modern urban life. This would not be easy: it meant a double point of view

[49]

throughout, but as one could not have the simple romance and the social criticism at the same time, there
would have to be frequent transitions, and these would
have to be very artfully done. And I would have to
work out a story that could be enjoyed on two different
levels. No, it would not be at all easy, I concluded, as
I scribbled a note or two for what might or might not
be future whole chapters.

And I was right, I added from my armchair in the
hut where I had struggled with the thing all winter. I
would not have been in that hut at that hour if all had
gone swimmingly with this novel. There would have
been nothing to destroy, whereas here, at my elbow,
waiting to be popped into the stove, was a thick pile of
typed sheets. The novel was nearly done now, but it
was not quite the novel I planned in the train coming
west. It was, as usual, a wretched compromise between
my fine ambitious plan and my modest ability as a
novelist. When the last word would come to be written, the workman, who had been compelled to keep his
nose down to it all winter, would be pleased, but the
artist in me, who hopefully does the initial planning,
would by that time have quitted the scene in disgust. I
have never written a work of any size and scope yet that
did not seem to the better half of me simply a dreadful
botched job, another failure. It is only years afterwards,
when I have forgotten what the grand plan was, that I
can take a peep at the thing and be surprised that it is

fairly passable. This is one reason why creative work is not the fun it is thought to be. It has its high moments, but the general drift always seems to be towards failure. You disappoint yourself with sickening regularity. It is to conceal this that we put on such a bold front to the world. Take it or leave it, we cry, knowing already that we ourselves have left it.

This was easily the most comfortable train journey across the American continent that I had had. The trains were now air-conditioned, a great improvement; and they had been speeded up. I had no sense this time of making an immense effort to reach the West. The leagues of prairie flowed effortlessly under our wheels. Because I had done it all before and was busy with my plans, I did not stare much at the passing countryside; yet I was surprised all over again by the apparent appearance of poverty and the ugly sketchiness of so much of these states. Fifth Avenue and Chicago's Lakeside seem in another world. They belong to the America of legend, the place of uncounted wealth. But where are the signs of wealth along this railway track? What disguised riches are there in these tumbledown wooden shacks passing for houses, these unpaved roads and streets, these piles of old tin cans and rusting skeletons of automobiles? Whole villages look as if they would be dearly bought at five hundred dollars, drug store and all. These folk who stare from their old Fords at the level crossings, a yellow melancholy in their faces, do they know that they have inherited the earth? This is, of course, pioneer country still.

To English eyes the pioneering seems to begin a mile or two outside New York. Most things you see appear to be makeshift; they will do for this year; and next year perhaps we can move to California or Florida or into the city. Money has been poured out in Niagara cataracts in the big cities to build their towers. But if there is much money in the country between, then fifteen hundred miles of it are inhabited by misers. I have seen ghost mining towns in the West, towns that could not have had more than ten years of life, that were better built than scores of these little rural towns and villages. Does nobody expect to stay long in them? Are they all camping? Are these folk real farmers or nomads who have temporarily lost enterprise? I ask because I do not know, being nothing but a foreigner glancing out of a fast train. Possibly there is here a combination peculiarly suited to the American taste, like sausages and buckwheat cakes; what seems to me a startling and painful contrast, immense boulevards and steel towers in one place, and mud tracks and miserable little wooden huts in a thousand other places, may appear to the average good American, such as the late Mr. Brisbane and his readers, amusing and refreshing, one more proof that the American is the luckiest of all citizens. I can only wonder. In a popular magazine I found in one of these trains, Mary Roberts Rinehart, who ought to know, de-

[52]

clared with militant emphasis that American citizens had far more comfort than any other people in the world, past and present. I hope they have, for they deserve it. But as a stranger, going past at fifty miles an hour, I cannot understand how they contrive to extract all this solid comfort, beyond the dreams of the English and French, Dutch and Swedes, out of these wooden shacks and rutted roads, these ugly, rusty and paintless villages, icy in winter, dusty and glaring in summer, slushy in early spring, menaced by drought and flood and winds that blow away whole farms. It does not sound comfortable, and most of them do not look comfortable.

Is there some magic by means of which what seems to me a heap of old tin cans and disused automobile parts appears to them something like an English cottage garden? Are the more intelligent novelists who write of these regions with a most depressing vividness merely so many liars? Do these people flee to the coasts or go wandering in homemade caravans because they rebel against so much comfort? True, all America is not here; but nevertheless it takes you about two days and nights, paying extra charges for fast travel, to put an end to it. And when I have gone north and south from this railway line, I have found nothing very different. It has always looked like a country on which not enough money has been spent, a doubtful and temporary habitation of our race.

There was time to notice people again. At the larger

stations, two contrasting types: the office man, the fellow caught in the net of business, usually pasty-faced, spectacled, worried, driven too hard by competition, salesmanship slogans, graphs of output, pep talks, all kinds of bullying, greedy rubbish; and the outdoor workingman—the truck-drivers, the railway men, and so forth—who looked superior to the men doing the same kind of work in Europe, big fellows in blue overalls, Whitman-ish lads, carrying themselves like free men, doing the job but not worrying too much, not caring a damn, and probably better off as husbands than the business men.

Comfort or no comfort, there is not much wrong with these workmen. One associates them with America's boldest and most triumphant enterprises, those colossal feats of civil engineering and large-scale building that seem to be the foundations of a new civilization. On their level, America is all that Arthur Brisbane and Mary Roberts Rinehart could claim for it. In this unconscious thrust through steel and stone, there is startling greatness. The wise European knows that here he is in the presence of something too big and new for him to grasp. To sneer is to diminish yourself. Probably we have been disappointed in America because we look in the wrong direction for its marks of noble achievement. We look for arts and philosophies when we should be looking at the new office building, the new bridge or highway; and we look for a few great men in the old way, artists and philosophers and scholars, when we should be looking at the thousands of new common men who mixed the concrete and threw the rivets.

These workmen, whose labor is mostly in the open air, have not been bleached and petrified as so many of the sedentary American men have been. I noticed that the manager of the dining-car had the face of a blanched red Indian. I have often noticed this kind of face on middle-aged American men. There may be something about the climate that carves this standard set of features. It turned the round Mongolian faces of the original natives into the long bony front of the red Indian. This manager looked anxious, without sap, clean out of key with a rich animal life, and sharply unlike his Negro waiters, who looked easy, vital, happily at home with their instincts. No doubt the Negroes had been hand-picked for the job, whereas the white man was an ordinary specimen of his kind. And then again, the white man had some responsibility—he looked as if he had half the weight of the world on his shoulders—and the Negro waiters had little or none. But even when all excuses had been made, it was hard not to feel that the slaves had won, after all. They had kept something rich and vital that had been worried and bullied and dried out of their white boss.

Some of the women in the dining-car irritated me. They always have done; perhaps they always will. The complaint is unchivalrous and not very reasonable, perhaps, but I cannot suppress it. These American women of a certain type which I see on the trains irritate me because they are dolled up all the time. Even at breakfast, you would think they were going to a party. Probably they consider they are at a party and that I am a lout to grumble because I am also at the party. But I am always wishing they would look plain and sloppy just for a change. Why be so aggressively feminine day and night? Why not relax, let up? A few wrinkles, a washed pale cheek, a mouth without lipstick, comfortable old clothes—in short, an appearance "like nothing on earth"—how welcome a sight that would be, especially over the orange juice in the early morning, at least to one traveling Englishman, perhaps homesick for his native frumpiness. Handsome young women would still look handsome young women if they appeared as God made them most of the day, and even if they didn't, that would be no great loss for a morning or two. It is not necessary to be handsome all the time; even the film stars take days off. As for the middle-aged and elderly women, what are they doing in dining-cars, at nine in the morning, so heavily made up that their faces are as hard as masks in the clear sunlight? They are doing it, no doubt, to please us all, to keep their end up; but they are not pleasing us. Nobody wants to see those masks in the morning sunlight. And there is one type of elderly American woman who looks terrifying to me. She has cotton-white and elaborately waved hair; all the honest lines have been blotted out of her face, except just here and there where the powder lies thick like snow in a mountain crevice; her mouth is small, grim, and incongruously scarlet; and usually she wears something fancy in the way of spectacles or eyeglasses. At a quick first glance, this type of woman looks like a distinguished specimen of American motherhood, perhaps intellectual and public-spirited, but also the sweet and gentle guardian of the hearth. After another glance or two, she begins to look stupid, intolerant, uncompromising, and sometimes downright cruel; all desiccated in her womanhood; a whitened tyrant; ready to hound you out of the county if you should be more generous-minded than she is and have the courage to prove it. Are there many women really like that, or is it that their desperate efforts to look their horrid best make many gentle and charming elderly women falsely accuse themselves?

The vitality, courage, and enterprise of American women are famous, needing no words from me. But how they must have to draw on these qualities! It is a bad business being a woman in most places, but in the United States it must be hell. No relaxation. No letting up for a second. Never relieved from the front-line trenches. Never dropping out of the race till Death rings the bell. I was thinking this in the train, but I had been observing literature rather than life. I had, in fact, been looking through some popular magazines, those cunning arrangements of advertisements with a little obvious fiction trickling through them. The copy in these advertisements was the literature that told me so much about American women. Most of my American friends laugh at this advertisement copy, as if it had nothing to do with the real America. I cannot believe that. The men and women in the advertising business must have an excellent knowledge of the public mind. Vast fortunes would not be spent on mere hazy guesswork. It is a knowledge severely tested by results.

These advertisements in the popular magazines tell one far more than the stories and articles they break into such irritating fragments. They showed me very clearly that the ordinary American woman, whose custom they are soliciting, is an unusually competitive being. She has only been freed from most of the drudgery of the European woman in order to lead a still more strenuous life. She has to compete all the time. When she is young she must look prettier than the girls she is with, otherwise the young males will ignore her completely. In my forty-odd years I have never yet been at any social function where all the young men crowded around one girl and left her less dazzling sisters to droop alone, but according to the advertisers this is always liable to happen in America, where the young males have a strange uniformity of taste, and a girl must either dazzle or be ignored. She must get her man. Then, having got him, she must keep him; and if she is not very careful—in various horribly intimate matters—she will not keep him. She has only to slack off for a day or two—and he has gone. If he does not go, and she marries him, then there may be children, and with them a whole host of new and terrible dangers. Mother must know, Mother must see to it, Mother must not grow careless for a moment. Suppose the children are doing well, can she afford to take it easy? No, no. She must serve the right kind of food, surround herself with the right kind of household appointments, go to the right places, read the right books; juggle with kitchen, coquetry, and culture; cultivate her body, cultivate poise, cultivate charm, cultivate personality, cultivate her mind.

Even though you can occasionally relax into the perfectly adjusted easy-chair or on the super-de-luxe mattress, with the acids and alkaloids inside you behaving themselves perfectly, it remains a hard life. Short of being President, no man would undertake to keep it up for four years. If they would let me off half of it, I would willingly go back to old-fashioned slopping about in the kitchen. But American women, it seems, cannot retreat. They must go on and on—you can see the goal gleaming in their eyes—but where exactly it is they are going the rest of us do not know. But if they should occasionally look worried, be intolerant and hard with their slack men folk, we cannot blame them. Not, that is, if the advertisements are true.

[59]

I remembered then what had happened when we had come this way the autumn before. I had described the journey for *Harpers Magazine*, and now had a copy of what I had written in my bag. This is how it went, beginning in Kansas. "There was a fine series of landscapes unrolling itself outside. The sky was a darkish gray-blue, and the trees in the distance, probably cotton-woods, showed light against it. The autumn foliage flared gorgeously in the occasional copses. These were watercolor landscapes. De Windt, who was at his best in this spacious autumnal country and season, would have done them exquisitely. Where is the De Windt of Kansas? Is he already there, staring at the scene?" (I was told afterwards that he was, but did not agree when I saw the work. But we do not know how many Kansas boys, now buried in obscure farms, may already be cherishing the seed of a talent greater than De Windt's. I believe that this state of great plains and skies may produce great painters yet. It took the Low Countries hundreds of years to produce theirs. God knows what may come out of America when the time is ripe.) "All this Middle West, with its huge arch of sky and its enormous distances, is painters' country. I know the novelists of the region, who are already achieving something of the mournful fatalism that comes from such vast plains, but I do not know the painters." (Do I really know the novelists, for that matter? I doubt it.) "And I think I would rather see my Middle West interpreted in paint than in words. Yet it was amusing to remember how delighted we were when we caught sight of a broad yellow river and were told it was the Missouri. That was because we knew and loved our Mark Twain, and felt that this rather depressing-looking river was really an old friend. We were of course a long way from the Huck Finn region, but, nevertheless, we felt that the immortal lad was only around the corner.

"Broken old railway cars, skeletons of automobiles, heaps of rusted tin cans, went past the windows, and then a town, a city—Kansas City. These heaps of scrap iron are a melancholy sight, but perhaps it will be a sad day when they are all tidied away, for it will mean that America is no longer a new country. There was a longish halt at Kansas City, so we left the station, and in clear sunlight we climbed the hill opposite to look at the enormous War Memorial, at which men were still working. With its raised platforms, fountains, twin museums, and tall tower, it is a dignified affair, very well designed, and I hope I shall be forgiven if I say that it seemed to me a waste of money." (Here I must break in to exclaim in wonder at the life we lead, we roving authors, just going around pointing out other people's mistakes. What have I to do with the Kansas City War Memorial? I wasn't asked to pay for it, was I? It's downright busy-bodying.) "Perhaps I have seen too many War Memorials; but I could not help feeling that

[61]

Kansas City could easily have found something better to celebrate than its participation in the Great War. Unless I am mistaken, this city played no small part in the opening of the West (it was here that the original Texan cowboys drove their vast herds of Longhorns, and so began the epic of the lariat), and a native theme of this kind would have been better worth celebrating in stone than the slaughtering of a few weary German machine-gunners. Pershing, Beatty, Foch, Diaz, all came here, and their heads have been carved on the Memorial walls; but in a few years who will care about these bemedaled heroes?" (These are still my sentiments. Most of the war reputations were vastly inflated, anyhow, and Kansas City was particularly unlucky in its choice of heroes.) "I went through the two museums, with their bits and pieces of war souvenirs, and thought them a waste of good masonry and roofing. If there is ever a movement in Kansas City to transform that Memorial into a monument of peaceful progress in America, celebrating the opening of the great West, that movement can count on the support of at least one English writer, who has seen enough stone carved to the glory of that tragic farce in France." (True, but what an unfortunate, conceited way of putting it. Some day, one of us will be lynched, and it will serve us right.)

"So, back to the train, where I discovered that the barber was a Scotsman, a shrewd little chap. He lived,

[62]

when not shaving passengers between Illinois and California, in Chicago, and in spite of the depression and the taxes, he had not the least desire to return to Scotland. I met several like him, men who would return to my island for a holiday but preferred working and living in America. And I could not, did not, blame them." (Which, you will admit, is durned good of me!)

To continue the quotation, now on its last lap: "Next morning we awoke in New Mexico, with the desert flashing past our windows and blue mountains on the horizon. The country was glorious. The villages were of an appalling hideousness. We had caught a glimpse or two of this country in films, but the acquaintance was very superficial. Why have the films left it so superficial? Nearly every person you saw along the route was a godsend as a film type, just as nearly every passing bit of landscape would have made an ambitious film director cry with envy. Yet how little has been done with this country! We have seen nothing of it except as a background to a few trumpery melodramas. New Mexico—what a film you could make out of it, not with handsome leading men and doll-faced actresses, but with the real people here, the wrinkled ranchers, the somber Mexicans, the mysterious Indians, the desert and the rocks and the shafts of sunlight! I was busy inventing a long speech to my friends in Hollywood on this theme, when there was a buzz at the door of our compartment, and I opened it to find a young lady in

[63]

fancy dress smiling at me. She referred me to the hand-bill we had already received, about the Indian Detour. I told her we should like to take the little trip. 'So glad you've talked it over,' she replied brightly, as if we had been sitting solemnly in committee on the subject. So she took about a dozen of us, including a little Chicago Jew who made bad jokes all the time, in a bus through Albuquerque, where, she explained, oddly, the chief trade was in 'health-seekers' and the manufacture of coffins and tombstones—a sinister conjunction. We ar-rived at the pueblo and had the embarrassment of wan-dering like mad sheep through other people's homes. Our guide, all smiles and enthusiasm (though the Chi-cago Jew tried her hard), explained how these Indians lived a happy communal life, almost entirely free from crime; and we representatives of the roaring, racketeer-ing world outside stared at the plump mahogany women and the children that looked like Chinese dolls. These Indian women lived by selling trinkets to staring tour-ists; their homes were perpetually on show; they be-longed to a dispossessed race; and yet the fact remains that they had a look of deep contentment not possessed by the female tourists, mostly elderly, who stared at them. Our guide explained that among these primitive folk the men still had a nasty trick of making the women do all the hard monotonous work, a fact that visibly scandalized the ladies of our party. A detached observer, comparing the two sets of women, might have come to the conclusion that for the females of our species there are certain things that more than compensate for an unfair share of the hard and monotonous work."

It was this contrast, and what I had written about it the year before, that I was remembering, after the advertisements had made me feel so sorry for the American woman, clamped into her competitive life. I could still see the two sets of faces: the white women, rather bony, arid, worried, and anxious, looking as if they were nervously scratching the surface of life; and the Indian women, with their sleepy fat smiles, sunk deep into an instinctive life as rich and satisfying as butter.

That self-torturing, terribly unhappy man of genius, D. H. Lawrence, came into my mind. He had been here in New Mexico once, as he had been in so many places, to praise the happy primitives. And he seemed to have had a bitter dislike of this very type of American woman, who is handled in several of his stories with the most savage cruelty. With an intensity I could never command and that I admire but somehow do not envy, Lawrence could have described that little scene in the pueblo so that it battered at your nerves, as everything seemed to batter at his. There would have been mysterious wild talk of the gods of the dark blood stream. He could have written fifty books about it, all quivering with prophetic indignation. Once again he would have shown us the prison we are in. But could he have laid a hand on the key to let us out? Did he ever let himself

out, except in the ecstasy of creation? What did his wan-
derings bring him, except new scenes to describe? Wasn't
he a man desperately wrestling with himself? He raged
against self-consciousness out of his own most elaborate
self-consciousness. He condemned us all, over and over
again, because we have "sex in the head" and not where
the primitive people keep it, in the body; and the charge
is true—we have sex in our heads now, and after we
have read Lawrence we have still more sex in the head
—and there is nothing to be done about it but boldly to
face the fact and make the best of it. The fatal contra-
dictions multiply themselves. The only genuine primitive authors are those who write happily for schoolboys
or young servant girls. Here is a man, in the midst of an
applauding circle of intellectuals, thundering against the
intellect. It will not do. It is a manifest absurdity to
write books in praise of illiteracy. To use the machinery
of industrial civilization—as a writer must do—in order
to proclaim the uselessness of the machinery of industrial civilization—this is cheating. We cannot be primitive, we can only play at being primitive, and are likely
to look silly while we are doing it. There was nothing
fatuous about Lawrence himself, for we see in him the
age-old tragic spectacle of the original genius, condemned to be misunderstood, reviled, driven out, sick
and suffering; but most of us cannot help finding something very fatuous about his little circle of highly self-

conscious and quarrelsome devotees, those intense arty ladies, wrangling from Taos to Bandol.

What are the plain facts in this disturbing contrast between the Indian women and the American? Surely, these. On their own level of life the Indian women have achieved a poise and a satisfying rhythm that the American women, on another level of life, have lost or not yet found. The American way of life has superseded the Indian, reducing it to a side-show, without real responsibility. There is no returning from one level to the other. These are old days to the Indian, but new and experimental ones to the American. And the way out for us lies ahead, not in less self-consciousness, but in more of it, a truer and deeper form of it. We must not run away from school, but stay longer at a better school. Somewhere around the corner is a happy and satisfying American life that must inevitably be quite different from the Indian's. It is by solving our own peculiar problems—and not by turning away and pretending they are not there—that we shall achieve our own right rhythm and poise, as the Indian long ago in his miniature world achieved his.

We have created an intricate social machinery to serve us, and now it is no longer serving us properly, but is bruising and tearing at us. Behind the querulous dissatisfaction of those American women was not the lack of some secret possessed by the Indians, but the aches and pains inflicted on them by this faulty organization.

Evil circumstances drove Lawrence out of his class and his country; he tried to forget both of them, but couldn't; so he maintained angrily that all this talk of the social structure of our modern life was idle and false; politics and economics and the elaborate network of conventions they wove were of no importance; all that mattered was the deep relationship between persons, a kind of blood brotherhood that any savage understood, and this relationship was unaffected by the social structure.

Let those American women, looking for guidance, follow him if they will. In the world revealed by his fiction, with its quivering nerves, its dark tides of blood, its gigantic impulses of fear, hate, love, they will find something deeply feminine, perhaps deeply satisfying. But he will guide them around a long and painful circle, and when they have come back to where they started from, perhaps to that very pueblo, they will still see the fat sleepy smiles of the Indian women, unattainable, mocking. Our surest reply to the challenge of those smiles is the eager question of the ethnologist or anthropologist, the delighted glance of the artist, even the grin of the traveling author, who sees in the contrast between these faces matter for another page and one more point to be scored.

I remembered then, turning it over as I sat in my little hut on the ranch in Arizona, that because I had begun thinking and arguing with invisible debaters again, I forgot the wounds that those telegrams about my play had dealt me on the windy platform of Albuquerque station. I had licked them hard, deep in self-pity, as the train groaned through the cold night among the mountains and marvels, the petrified forests and picture rocks, the giant craters and dinosaurs' footprints, of northern Arizona. For an hour or two I was not traveling in any country. I was motionless and alone, with that immense vanity, which is the scribbler's curse, raging now like a fever; the children of my tenderest fancy had just been massacred by half-wits; my most intimate confidences had been answered by yawns; eyes glazed with boredom had stared contemptuously at scenes dear to me; my gift had been rejected, flung into my face. All an author's eggs, every precious one of them, are in one basket. Kick it away and you spill and break on the ground his livelihood, all his hope, his self-respect; one blow—and they seem to him to be lost forever. He feels ruined down to the last cell. If you do not want his work, then there is nothing of him you want: he is as good as dead. He burned all his boats long ago—did not leave himself time and interest enough to build the smallest raft—and so he is lost.

But then, miraculously, he suddenly finds himself again. The first numbed feeling soon disappears. He is angry, and begins arguing passionately with all the fools who will not understand. And in these arguments, idiotic though they are, his mind comes to life again, soon stops traveling in the dreary circle of self-interest, fastens on the world, the great round fat world, and all is well. Or as well as it can be. So when I awoke next morning, to see the sun of California, my wounds were healing fast. It was a damned shame about the play, that's all.

And now, months afterwards, as I remembered these things, I told myself that it was still a damned shame, but I said it without heat, and found I had not even a scar where I thought once I was bleeding to death. I stretched out my feet to the stove, retraced my steps into this recent but now involved labyrinth of memory; and I picked myself up at the end of the previous October, arriving in California to meet my family, who had come around by sea, and to begin our winter in the West.

Chapter Four

AFTER I had met my family in San Pedro, we had not gone straight to the Arizona ranch where we were to spend the winter, but had put in two or three weeks at a guest ranch near Victorville on the Mohave Desert. I remembered this, but only mechanically at first, as one recalls a time-table of travel. For a minute or two, only names returned to memory, not a single image of the country, the ranch itself, our fellow guests there. I had to make an effort to find myself again on the Mohave Desert. We had used that Californian ranch merely as a halting-place on the way to Arizona, to give the children a rest after the long voyage from England. And I was struggling hard to begin my novel.

I am one of those writers who begin slowly, hesitantly, badly. I do not like making that first step, which I always feel is decisive, compelling me for the rest of the narrative to move steadily in one direction. My novels may not seem—in fact, I know by this time that they certainly do not seem—closely knit, severely logical in their action, yet that is how they appear to me, I suppose; otherwise I would begin them easily, gayly, and only find them difficult later on when the first rush of improvisation had slackened. As it is, I begin slowly and dubiously, and gather confidence and speed as I go on, usually ending with a fine flourish. Even with plays, where the third act is ten times as hard to write as the first, I hesitate to begin, but am traveling easily when the final curtain is in sight. It seems as if such creative powers as I possess work like the internal-combustion engine. (Probably there is somebody writing a book at this moment to prove there is very little difference between such powers and the engine that has begun to dominate our lives.)

The fact remains that at that ranch near Victorville, what happened between me and my portable typewriter upstairs was more real, has remained longer in my memory, than my life there outside working-hours.

I remember, however, that we found the Mohave Desert disappointing, much inferior to its Arizona neighbor at that season. This southern California desert is more like the conventional idea of a desert than that in Arizona, and the film people in Hollywood have made great use of it. Out there, just beyond the Cajon Pass, the handsome lads of the Foreign Legion have marched to their death, for the sake of a woman and Warner Bros. The ranch looked out on very bare country, though there was a genuine river flowing through the valley, with willows and cottonwoods along its banks. Away from the river, though, there was nothing but the sinister Joshua tree (a kind of yucca) and the stunted growths of mesquite and creosote. Except in the brief glory of sunset and the afterglow, the surrounding mountains looked desolate, sullen, inhospitable. We did not take to this desert. It seemed, at that season, to lack color and mystery, an arid and unfriendly country. Nearly all the time we were there a bitter wind raked the dunes, making lounging impossible and walking unpleasant. There was plenty of sunshine, but this cold, gusty, gritty wind would not let us alone to enjoy it. You looked through a window at the ranch and saw the mountains and desert apparently baking in the sun, but once you were actually out, you were caught by this cruel wind, which promptly gave you a headache. There has always been to me something oddly sinister about a strong wind blowing beneath a clear sky. I do not think I found this section of the Mohave Desert downright frightening, but I never made friends with it. I was never sorry to get back to the pleasant adobe ranch house, even if it meant that I must resume my struggle with the novel.

Most of the other guests there were from Hollywood, directors and actors and their wives who wanted a short rest, or had been ordered to take a child away from the coast for a time. They were not the very rich and fashionable Hollywood folk, for they generally go to Palm Springs and Jacinto, where they can enjoy that complete privacy they so much desire entirely surrounded by photographers and publicity men. Our lot were mostly hard-working and not very fancy film folk.

The one I remembered best was a little assistant-director, whose dark little wife, of Italian parentage, and his miniature daughter, had been sent out to the desert for a period by the doctor. Whenever the studio let him go, he burned up the miles between Hollywood and Victorville, coming and going at all odd times of day and night. Sometimes the studio called him back before he had had time to finish a meal at the ranch. Cursing the whole film industry, he would embrace his two sparkling little brunettes, shout a good-by to us all, and go roaring back over the mountains. He was a short, thick-set chap in his early forties, very tough, but friendly and likable and immensely entertaining. He came from Brooklyn or the Bronx, had knocked about a bit, and got into the picture game early, first as a news-reel cameraman. He was the kind of man that Hollywood scenario-writers, who have often come out of the same tough school, like to make the central figure of their screen stories: very masculine, courageous, kind-hearted, devoted to his womenfolk and his pals, senti-mental about a few things, but entirely disillusioned about or indifferent to a great many other things. We have met his kind in American films, plays, novels, over and over again. He is, indeed, a very American type.

I remembered him best not simply because I found

his reminiscences so entertaining, but because so much of what he told me seemed to me to throw a clear, hard light on an America I do not know directly. I do not mean that all his stories were about this America, but that somehow I kept getting glimpses of it as he talked. He did not belong to it himself. It is a world below that agreeable surface of genial acquaintances, excellent travel arrangements, and scrupulous hygiene, which the visitor knows. It is a world partly revealed by the newspapers, a world of racketeers and grafters, gunmen and pimps and molls, in which money is everything and the law and ordinary human decency are nothing, the police seem little better than a uniformed gang, millionaires are jealous and murderous caliphs, the frame-up is a neat device for embarrassing the other fellow, and everybody and everything have their price. It is not a tropical underworld of hot blood and passion, of people too barbaric for the bourgeois virtues. It is a chilly, gray, cellar-like, fungus world, of greed, calculated violence, and a cold sensuality. The more austere writers of American detective stories, such as Dashiel Hammett, seem to show us that world. Its doings can apparently only be described in short staccato sentences. "I had five more drinks. Then I kicked the old man in the guts. After that I went upstairs and threw the blonde on the bed." As if we were receiving telegrams from this chilly dank hell.

How big is this particular America? Does it exist in

only a few big cities? And if there is not much of it, why do we hear so much about it? I find distinct traces of it, for example, in fiction that is not intended to be easy sensational stuff. In Dos Passos, for instance. In many of the younger novelists of urban life. And, of course, the films have given us great slabs of it, mutilated here and there by the censors. It makes no appearance that I know of in the fiction of yesterday. It does not show up even in the work of a tough-minded realist like Frank Norris. It belongs, then, to contemporary America. It came out of the War, Prohibition, the Depression, or what you will. And whatever its size, it is ever so much bigger than the little Chicago-Sicilian-Irish gang world, with which it must not be confused. It is not necessary to furnish this larger hell with gangsters and Thompson sub-machine guns. You could show it flourishing without a single trigger being pulled. A cold corruption is the mark of it. Yet honor and decency and affection do not seem to have rotted down there; they would appear to have never existed. Its inhabitants are so many talking wolves.

I was not mollycoddled in my childhood; I have been through a long war; I have seen and endured a good deal in my time; and I do not mind saying that the very existence of this world I have described appalls me. No threat out of it has ever come my way; no friend of mine has ever been slugged to death down one of its dark alleys; yet I am profoundly disturbed by the thought of its very existence. Perhaps I am fussing about nothing. Neither the writers nor their readers seem to worry. Yet I feel that if I lived in America I should be wondering all the time if one wrong turning might not bring me into this frozen forest, with its packs of human wolves, if any day a door might not close behind me, completely shutting out the clean sunlight and every civic virtue that has ever been generated by it. All this may seem merely fanciful. Let us get down, as they say, to cases. Some of these stories I heard that seemed to throw a light on this strange sub-world told me how very rich men had rid themselves of people they disliked, sometimes by having them "framed" and then sent to prison, sometimes by outright murder. The fact that such stories are told one over and over again, by all manner of persons, does not prove that they are true. But if only some of them are true, then I feel that if I lived in America I should want to know what to do. I might have to keep reminding myself: Now here is a very rich man, be careful you don't offend him, for you know what might happen. Nothing very fanciful about that. Just necessary plain rules of conduct. Yet a great many very rich men are unpleasant, and it might be difficult to be conciliatory all the time. What then? Do I go into hiding, or leave the country?

Any decent citizen who protests at this point that it is all a pack of nonsense has my sympathy. I hope he is right, and that the fiction-writers, the journalists, and the tough story-tellers are wrong. Yet it seems unlikely they would all combine to invent this bestial underworld, just for fun. And queer things do happen: people disappear mysteriously; bodies are found. They happen in England, too, but nothing like so frequently. And when they do happen in England, there are not all the winks and nudges and hints of what the "low-down" might be.

Only a few weeks after I left the Mohave Desert, I remembered, I was in Hollywood when the body of Thelma Todd, the film actress, was discovered in the roadhouse she ran, out on the road to Malibu. I did not remember what the final official verdict was, but I did remember a thousand queer disconcerting hints and whispers and guesses. It was as if, for a moment, a gulf had opened, almost at one's feet, and there had come from it the stench of decay and death. In that atmosphere of suspicion it was hard not to feel that the wretched girl, once so pretty and lively, had been suddenly dragged into this immense pit and then hurled back into the sunlight again, a corpse. Possibly the real truth about it was quite simple, something that might have happened to such a girl in any country, but it is easy to doubt it. Too many hints, whispers, queer stories. Too much smoke altogether for there to be no fire at all.

The main ranch house on the Mohave Desert had a fine big sitting-room, with a wooden gallery and rafters, adobe walls hung with pictures and Indian rugs, and an enormous brick open fireplace. Here we would sit up late, this little man from Hollywood, happy to be under the same roof again with his merry little wife and pretty child, and myself, lounging at ease and curious to hear, after my day's work. And as we smoked, he would tell me his tales of horror, not to make my flesh creep, but merely to show that it was a queer world, this we were in, and that there were some very unpleasant things that could happen in it. When I grew indignant, he agreed with my indignation, but obviously he took such horrors for granted, as an Eskimo might regard his long sunless winter. Graft, perjury, corruption, murder, these were to him among the realities, the given conditions, of life. While denouncing the morals of the people in this sub-world, he did not seem to question its right to exist at all. It did not seem to occur to him that it ought to be suppressed like an outbreak of plague. I feel sure that if I had been an American and had announced that I was campaigning fiercely against such evils, he would have regarded me with suspicion, as a fanatic, a radical, a Red. Yet he was anything but a fool, a coward, a knave, himself. His trouble, I think, was that he was incapable of considering the social scheme of things. The definition of Man as a political animal did not apply to him. In everything else fully adult, he was politically about ten years of age. Or he might be compared to an old-fashioned woman, though whole hordes of apparently new-fashioned young women are not very different. Like them, he saw quite recent political and social growths as unalterable natural features in our life, no more to be challenged than the trees and rocks in a landscape. Thus his cynicism was the finest possible protection for everything that he knew was wrong. Under that knowing glance and shrug, it could flourish forever. If the fools and cowards give in, and those who are stronger and wiser accept, merely keeping a sharper eye on their own affairs, then this cold hell can fatten itself and spawn unchecked. It was his country, and it was not for me to tell him how to manage it. But sometimes, as I sat there listening, the late hour pricking my imagination, I could see glistening tentacles wreathing up from that pit towards the sleeping children upstairs, and had to shake myself out of a shuddering nightmare.

All this I remembered, while the memory of many pleasant things, the mountains in the afterglow, the picnic suppers at the ranch, the good talks we had, was already ghostly. And then I recollected something else, a tiny absurdity. They kept fifty or sixty turkeys in a corral a few hundred feet away from the ranch house, and one of my children discovered that if she went up to their fence and cried at the top of her voice "All together, boys!" they would look up as one bird and instantly and loudly reply, *Gobble-gobble-gobble*. After that we all tried it, with varying success, but the original discoverer never failed to obtain the maximum result, an instant and unanimous *Gobble-gobble-gobble.* I could see and hear again those solemn and idiotic birds, all their faces turned towards us, so eagerly expectant of the food we could not give them, all their voices raised in chorus. And I thought, not very cheerfully, that if she cared to develop on those lines, with that technique, that child of mine had the makings of a very successful politician. After all, what is it we are always hearing and reading, in talk, at public meetings, in the newspapers? *Gobble-gobble-gobble.*

Chapter Five

IT WAS with almost a sense of home-coming that we left the Mohave Desert for the ranch near Wickenburg, Arizona, where we had stayed the winter before. We sent our heavy baggage by train, but did the journey ourselves by car. I came to know that road from California to Arizona very well; this was my third trip along it, and before the winter was over I had made a great many more. You descend from the orange and vine districts, which, with their dazzling fruit and the snowy peaks above, are so blatantly picturesque, so vulgarly confident in their appeal, that your mind blankly refuses to welcome any image of them, down and down, below sea-level, to the sheer desert, bare as Arabia, around the Salton Sea, where the infrequent filling-stations, tiny oases of water and gasoline, have home-grown dates for sale. Even in winter it is very warm down in this desert; in summer it must be sizzling.

The Salton Sea is a fantastic sheet of water. It is a great basin fifty miles long, and was once an arm of the Gulf of California. Then for ages it was nothing but a vast bed of salt. But in 1905 the Colorado River, whose antics are now controlled by Boulder Dam, broke all bounds, and for two years poured itself into this basin, to form a strange inland sea, younger than most police sergeants. The main highway between the two states now passes north of the Salton Sea, but I was fond of making a detour that brought us close to it.

What fascinated me—and still fascinates me, so that I know that very soon I shall have to go that way again —was the utter desolation of the scene here. I would ask whoever was driving me to wait behind with the car while I walked forward a mile or so. The only sound in the world was that of my footfalls. If I stopped, then the only sound was my breathing. I do not mean that it was quiet there: it was absolutely silent. Not a bird, not an insect. One bumblebee could have shattered that crystal of quiet like a squadron of bombing planes. But it remained inviolate. One might have been on a dead planet. There was the Salton Sea; there was the desert; under a sky like a luminous metal lid. Nothing else. Water, stone, and air. If you want to return to one of the earlier ages of geological time, walk for a few minutes by the Salton Sea. You will be fascinated, and secretly frightened. Here is a glimpse at once of the beginning and end of us. This is how the world was before we began to trouble it, and this is how it may be when the last man has looked reproachfully at the fading sun, cursed the freezing universe, and died. A trip in Wells' Time Machine. In a few minutes it is all over. The car you left behind comes roaring down at you; and voices, your own among them, a magical babble, are heard again; and the sounding stream of life bears you away. But you will remember. Whenever there comes a deep silence, the memory of this still deeper silence, the eternal zero, will return to your mind, to challenge it.

Time after time, along these desert roads, from here as far north as the entrance to Death Valley, we were entranced and bewildered by mirages. First the mountains would blur and then change their outlines; great bastions would dissolve; peaks would fade like smoke; whole ranges would waver and drift; as if Doomsday had quietly dawned. It was like looking at a landscape with a four-dimensional eye. Then the desert itself would turn illusionist. In the distance it would quiver and wink in the strong sunlight, and then, like a dissolve in a film, the arid ocher stretches would glassily darken and then dapple themselves, and lakes would appear, exquisite cool lakes, fringed with trees clearly reflected in the depths, and you would swear that there were houses among the trees and boats on the water. One moment you were staring through the windshield at this witchery of green leaves and blue water, and then the next moment it had all gone and there was nothing there but the desert, quivering and winking again. I was told that some people here had plainly seen ships in the sky, perhaps reflected from the Pacific hundreds of miles away, but this I never saw, though I must have seen scores of most convincing lake mirages. Rushing through the desert, towards ample supplies of water and food, at seventy miles an hour, one could afford to be idly amused by this odd magic, but to the early settlers, moving so slowly and laboriously on foot or wagon, praying for water, these mirages must have seemed a hellish trick, the conjuring of the devil himself. To see those depths of water, those lovely trees, turn into rock and sand! How those infernal dissolves must have called out the last resources of faith and courage and endurance! What men and women, what a history, what a country! And all happening yesterday.

I had thought many a time of these sharp contrasts in travel, all this amazing development, yet I thought of them once more, as I smoked this midnight pipe in my hut. The road I had traveled so often between California and Arizona is so recent that it is not marked in all its length even on many new maps. It was only in 1910 that Arizona was incorporated into the Union as a separate state. Everything that happened here before yesterday is prehistorical. Turn back a page or two, and the Indians are raiding, the bad men are shooting up the towns, and the traveler whose horse has gone lame is dying of thirst. Middle-aged men can remember the time when these smooth broad state highways were faint trails. The very children have seen them being made. Yet these roads, running across mountains and deserts, now see a whole new world of travel and commerce and social life.

We in England tell ourselves that we have now brought back to our roads a brisk life they lost when the railways first came; but America, with its vaster distances, its greater restlessness, only stimulated by the depression, has easily outreached us. Here along these Western highways, with their fine surfaces, careful grading and banking, elaborate signs, their filling stations, their auto camps, their roadside eating-houses and hotels, their little towns passionately claiming your custom in a startling sudden glare of electric signs, is a brand-new busy world. It has its own inhabitants: the highway patrols; the wandering out-of-works "thumbing" you for a lift; the whole families traveling in old Fords grotesquely festooned with bedsteads and frying-pans; the uniformed lads at the filling stations; the C.C.C. boys, brown and grinning and very different from our own hollow-cheeked unemployed; the elderly retired couples moving sedately in their motor caravans. A contemporary American *Don Quixote*, *Gil Blas*, or *Tom Jones* could be written about these highways and their people.

The lads and men at the filling stations always caught my eye, they were so different from the sleepy, perfunctory fellows who work the pumps in England. Here they fill your tanks as if they had dedicated their lives to a great mission. They are, proudly, passionately, filling-station experts. They hasten to clean your wind-shield, to offer water, either for yourself or the radi-ator; they make zestful remarks about the day; they ask you to call again.

And every village and tiny town, with its neon signs, looks to a European like a bit of a city that has just detached itself. There are the drug stores, the eating-houses, the hotels, all blazing with colored lights. They may be a hundred miles from anywhere, deep in the desert, but you would imagine that somebody had con-trived to pick out a block from Sunset Boulevard, Los Angeles, and drop it down there. At night you travel either in the darkness of Siberia or through what ap-pears to be the main street of a carnival town. And you also notice at night, coming this way, the air beacons on the distant peaks, flashing red and white for the pilots of the transcontinental night planes. Everything here had no existence, would have meant nothing if it had been dreamed of, the day before yesterday. It is all today's doing. It is all bright-new. And most of it, in its pretty frivolity of colored lights and facetious appeals, seems to have no more to do with the savage countryside itself than a jiggling line of chorus girls would have. Yet these toylike arrangements were con-ducting us, up in the air as well as on the ground, straight across the waterless wilderness, day and night.

I reflected then that all this, new as it was, could not be regarded as a solitary experiment, a local eccentricity.

[87]

I knew I should find something like it all over these United States. By day, by night, private cars and giant buses go roaring out from New York away across the continent to San Francisco and Los Angeles, with the planes shooting past them like aluminum projectiles. Very soon there would be something like this road life all over the world, penetrating Africa, glittering across Asia. *Gas, Eats, Hot and Cold Drinks:* something like this would be spelled out, in paint by day, in neon lights after dark, all the way from Shanghai to Cape Town. There was rapidly coming into existence a new way of living—fast, crude, vivid—perhaps a new civilization, perhaps another barbaric age—and here were the signs of it, trivial enough in themselves, but pointing to the most profound changes, to huge bloodless revolutions.

There had been no planning. Some people took to moving here and there, others hurried along the roads they went to make a few dollars; that was all. Perhaps there would not be any planning for a long time, until it would be too late to plan. This new life was simply breaking through the old like a crocus through the wintry crust of earth. And it was here in America, and above all in this America of the Pacific Coast, that the signs of it were most multiplied and clearest.

America is definitely in front. She hardly knows she is leading us, but she is. Russia can turn the old economic and political system upside down, but no sooner has she done so than she takes a long look at America.

One country after another follows suit. They may be ten years behind, but they are following on steadily. America does not know where she is going, but if she walks into some abyss of barbarism, she will not walk alone. This, I concluded, was a solemn responsibility. Britain had a similar responsibility when she achieved her industrial revolution, and led the way to the slag-heaps and dirty back alleys and poisoned air, to the greed and cynical indifference of competitive industrialism. So far she has failed the world, for having led it into this dark pit, she has not yet led the way out. It is now America's turn.

If any American denies all this, adding that it is a queer lot of far-fetched stuff to come from the sight of a few gasoline stations, auto camps, new roads, and air beacons, I have no reply. I shall persist in my belief, however, that it is here in these States that the Time Spirit is working hardest, harder even than it is in Russia, and that American political and social ideas, though they are changing already, will have to bound forward, to borrow some of the enterprise and courage of the engineers and builders and even of this new wayside population, in order to keep up. In short, you will have to discover where it is you are taking us.

Chapter Six

ARIZONA, to which we had now returned, had been first recommended to us, as a place with a superb winter climate, by John Galsworthy, who used to come here, winter after winter. One of us had been ordered by her doctor to keep well away from the damp, cold, and fog that regularly besiege London from November to March, and so, after a preliminary visit by two of us, now the whole lot of us were there. I think our chosen district, near Wickenburg, between Phœnix and Prescott, and about two thousand feet high, has the best winter climate in the state, which means that it has one of the best winter climates in the world, which is notoriously short of good winter climates. There are plenty of warm moist places—almost the whole range of the tropics—but not fairly warm dry ones. Here I prophesy that as transport becomes quicker, cheaper, easier, the Wickenburg district will become increasingly important, for a winter climate as good as this will prove a better gold-mine than the Old Vulture, which Henry Wickenburg discovered while chasing his burro, ever was. In short, there's gold in them thar hills, but the best of it is the January sunshine.

The air is enchanting, quite unlike any I have known before, being crystal clear and faintly but persistently aromatic. It is this air, strongly actinic, that gives the Arizona landscape its enduring charm. Seen close at hand, there is nothing very attractive about these hills, so prickly with cactus, or the savage rocky peaks behind them. There is no foreground prettiness here, as there is in California. The vast distances do the trick. This air seems to act like a powerful stereoscopic lens. Everything far away—and you can see scores of miles—is magically molded and colored. The mountains, solidly three-dimensional ranges and peaks, are an exquisite blue in the daytime, and then turn amethyst at sunset. Things near at hand are dusty green, grayish, brownish, rather drab, but everywhere towards the far horizon rise chunks of color, unbelievably sumptuous. And the nights are even more spacious than the days. No lid of darkness is clapped over you. The spaces are wider than ever, and are lit, night after night, with all the stars of the Northern Hemisphere, as precisely defined as the stars in a planetarium. To return to England is to feel like a man who is let down into a cellar after sunset. If Shakespeare had ever seen such nights of stars, he would have gone mad trying to improve upon his "Look, how the floor of heaven is thick inlaid with patines of bright gold!" But literature does not like too much encouragement, which is why some of the best lyrical poetry, ecstatic in its praise of nature, has

[91]

been written by fellows shivering and fog-bound in dark attics. No real poetry has come out of Arizona yet, and not much painting. Nature is doing it all.

Now that the bad men have shut up their last saloon and we tourists are coming into Arizona, the copy-writers in the publicity departments of the railways and the local chambers of commerce are showering their adjectives on the place and gushing over it like new oil-wells. These professional enthusiasts are ruining travel for us. No reality can hope to compete with their purple eruptions. It is no use going to a nice little pic-turesque place if you have already had such rhapsodies about it pumped into you. What is this real world after those shiny folders, probably called *Wondrous Trails of Sheer Romance?* One reason why even moderately intelligent people sink deeper and deeper into disillusion is that nothing now comes up to the advertisements. We know there are no such razors, such soaps, such cigars, such shoes and ships and sealing-wax. Few things are advertised at greater expense and with more cunning than travel. Any tourists' agent will give you an armful of pictures of an ideal world. The light that never was on land or sea, the consecration and the poet's dream, shine from these booklets. You can make the round trip, in solid comfort and with the nicest people, to half a dozen Utopias. Now Arizona is having its share of this glittering and deceptive nonsense. One of the mildest descriptions of it is *This Wonderland of the*

Great Southwest. This is enough to make any intelligent adult regard the place with the gravest suspicion. It must be a fraud on an impudently gigantic scale. And oddly enough, it isn't. For once these descriptions have an almost scientific precision. Nothing has been exaggerated. I am not a son of the state, have not ten cents invested in it, and am not being paid to boost it. Nevertheless, I declare that Arizona really is a wonderland. You ought to enter it by floating down a rabbit-hole.

It is filled with marvels. Wizardry has been at work here. In the north, where you are a mile and a half high, there is the Grand Canyon, which is enough in itself to clear a whole continent from the charge of being dull. But you also have the Painted Deserts and the Petrified Forests. The dinosaurs left their tracks in these parts. When the giant meteor decided to imbed itself in the earth, it chose Arizona, and you may see the crater it made, near Winslow. There are great tracts of virgin forest, as well as hundreds of miles of desert. There are mysterious Indian ruins all over the place. There are strange heights called the Superstition Mountains, where men have gone to look for lost gold-mines and have never returned. There is about the whole state a suggestion of the *Arabian Nights.* Its vegetation, with the immense pillars of Saguaro cactus dominating everything else, is fantastic. Its rocks hide treasures of gold, opals, and rubies, and are covered with ancient writing, perhaps Indian symbols for *Open Sesame.* Its moon,

[93]

stars, and mountain peaks seem to be burnished by *genii*. Sinbad might have once passed this way, and there may come a morning when a riding-party will find a new valley and there disturb the Roc himself.

The old-timers here—the stringy old cowboys still rolling their cigarettes—the withered and dusty prospectors sitting by their piles of empty bean-cans—sound like the most stupendous liars, but you cannot be sure that they are not indulgently descending into the truth, for anything might have happened, and still might happen, in this vast empty state. Take the wrong turning here one morning, and you might never be heard of again. But what might happen to you, nobody knows. The clever fellows who sit in Chicago writing those *Wonderland of the Southwest* railway folders, thinking how cunningly they are taking us in again, do not know the half of it. One day they will come and lose themselves in Arizona, and be heard screaming among the hills for new and impossible adjectives. The Baghdad barber and all his six brothers will turn up here, sooner or later, and Scheherazade herself will be discovered in the beauty parlor of the Adams Hotel, Phœnix. It is not for nothing that the capital of the state is called Phœnix. And if this town does not match your mood, you can try Yuma and Buckeye, Ajo and Nogales and Tombstone. This was the last state to enter the Union, and if it is not the most fantastic of them all, I will eat my hat and it shall be a ten-gallon Stetson.

It was here in Arizona that I first met cowboys. Many of these cowboys now spend more time taking parties of ranch guests out for a morning ride than they do in rounding up cattle. Nevertheless, they are genuine cowboys. As a rule they have known nothing but ranch life, and they have all the accomplishments of the legendary cowboy, except perhaps that famous marksmanship with a Colt. When not at work they practice for forthcoming rodeos or entertain themselves, and you, with that melancholy music, those long lugubrious strains, for which all men who lead an active open-air life seem to have a strange passion. Sedentary men may need gay cynical little tunes, but the cowboy, the sailor, the soldier, and their kind ask for nothing better than a gloomy ballad of true love cut short by early death. The cowboy, who is a man of tradition, keeps the traditional tone in song, an odd and rather nasal little tone, which would drive any singing-master mad but somehow pleases the rest of us.

And like all healthy primitive males, the cowboy is a dressy fellow. Most of his pay still goes, as it always did, in tremendous hats and high-heeled boots, in belts and saddles and gaudy shirts. He is a peacock of a chap, unimpressed by any defeatist urban nonsense about quiet, respectable, drab clothes. The male in his natural state likes to show off, to blind the coy female, to stun her into admiration; and that is the cowboy.

He has the luck to live in a simple world. There are

certain things he must be able to do well, or it is all up with him, and they cannot be faked, as politicians and professional men and directors of companies so often fake things. He cannot pretend to ride and rope, and get away with it. He has to be able to ride and rope really well, and to do a few other things, too; but once he has acquired the necessary skill, and the courage and endurance that match it, all is well with him. He lives a natural healthy life in a healthy uncomplicated world. He does not go to bed to worry himself sick about what the public, the debenture-holders, the board of directors, the departmental boss, will say. He does not feel like a piece of straw in a whirlpool. He does not grow fat and apoplectic, or thin and cancerous, at a desk, wondering what exactly it is that has wasted his manhood. He has not much money, but then neither has he many taxes, mortgages, insurance policies, and doctors' bills. If he has a wife, she does not regard him as a sagging, moody fraud of a fellow, whose mysterious and probably contemptible activities during the day have robbed him of all bright masculine virtue; but she knows exactly what he has to do, and respects him for the obvious skill and courage he brings to his tasks. If he has young children, he shines in their sight as a wise hero, and is therefore the perfect father. His life may be infinitely narrower than that of a saint or a philosopher, an artist or a scientist, but can it be said to be any narrower than the existences of all those pale-faced millions who go day after day to factories, warehouses, offices, and shops, the victims of all the cunningly deployed forces of publicity and salesmanship, of rubber-stamp opinions and artificially stimulated wants?

He is at peace with himself because his work allows free play to the strongest instincts of man. Unlike so many other men, he has not to pretend to be a short-sighted, deaf cripple all day to earn his living, and then to try and catch up with himself as a vital human being during the short hours of leisure allotted to him. His work is not without danger, and he is sustained by a sense of this, knowing that he has a certain fundamental dignity. This is true of other kinds of men, such as the miner and the sailor, men who are shabbily treated by the community they serve, but are often inwardly sustained by their sense of being engaged in an heroic calling. This is joined in the cowboy to an outward picturesqueness and a magnificent stage-setting.

There is still a good book to be written about the legend of the heroic West and the cowboy. The author would have to be a social philosopher as well as an historian. The legend has not been with us long. That West had a very short history. It did not begin until the 'sixties, and its Homeric age was over before the century ended. It was created by a passing set of economic circumstances, by cheap open grazing-land in the Southwest, and good prices on the hoof in Kansas City. It

[97]

could not survive the invention of barbed wire. Yet what a legend it has created!

Cheap melodrama, whether in fiction, plays, or films, soon claimed that legend; yet there always remains a faint gleam of Homeric poetry, not in the monotonous and incredible fables of very good men and very bad men and doll-like heroines, but in the enduring image they give us of a man riding in the wilderness of desert and mountain, the solitary heroic figure. Here is one who seems to have escaped the economic slavery and universal degradation of our time; who does not compete except with charging animals and the hostile elements; who is seen as the strong free male, careless and smiling and bronzed, that essential male for whom all women have a tenderness. He is a man of our world who has contrived to live his life in an epic simplicity impossible to the rest of us, caught in a bewildering tangle of interests and loyalties.

All this is more than enough to explain the flood of popular stories, plays, and films about the cowboy. They are not so good as he was or still is. There has rarely been a genuine artistic impulse behind these things. The material has nearly always been better than the workmen. Indeed, many of the workmen have had no respect for the material, turning it into so much commercial hokum. Thus, the cowboy and his West, the whole sunlit legend, have been cynically distilled into what the more impatient and austere critics of our society call "dope." The heroic free man, they will tell us, has been used to stupefy the enslaved masses. This is true. But we must ask ourselves what disease it is that these masses are suffering from that demands this particular form of dope. Are they entranced by the cowboy simply because they do not own the means of production, because they belong to the exploited proletariat, because the profits of their factories are being handed over to capitalist shareholders? Change all this, and does this wistful admiration of the cowboy vanish at once? I doubt it.

The disease is not so easily diagnosed. It is less general and superficial, more personal to each man and woman, cutting deeper into the psychic; though I will readily admit that the make-up of our personalities owes more to economic and political conditions, capable of being completely changed in a few years, than most of us care to acknowledge. A free people, no longer feeling obscurely but deeply that their lives were undignified, unheroic, a waste of manhood, but conscious of the fact that every stone they lifted would be set in its place in the city wall, would smile with pleasure at the sight of the lean graceful cowboy, but would not hunger for every doped confection offered under his name. Yet I believe some wistfulness would remain; the men with the machines, in their air-conditioned factories, would be haunted by the vague image of the man with the horse and the camp fire.

From the first moment we met the cowboy and his folk we were impressed by their manners. While you are still a stranger, the cowboy observes with you an almost Spanish punctilio. His polite questions have an air of grave concern. He does not, in the actors' term, "throw away" his *Please* and *Thank you*. He listens carefully to what you have to say, and may be brief but is never offhand in his replies. His manners are very much like those of old-fashioned Americans in most parts of the country.

It is odd that American men are so frequently presented in European caricatures of the type, in fiction, plays, and films, as being extremely ill-mannered, loud, rough customers. Such Americans exist, of course, just as sneering Englishmen, bullying Teutons, insolent Latins, also exist. But it has always seemed to me that American manners in general tend to err on the side of formality and solemnity. They are rather like those of elderly English dons and clergymen. The ordinary English are much more casual. We do not take enough trouble, for example, with our introductions. Terrified of appearing pompous, we hastily mumble names or hastily accept a mumble instead of names, so that our introductions do not serve their purpose, and often, not knowing to whom we are talking, we saunter into the most dreadful traps. The deliberate ceremony that most Americans make of introductions protects them from these dangers and errors.

I think the Far Western manner with strangers is like that which was common among all cultivated persons in the Eastern States a generation or two ago. But unless you deliberately make yourself unpleasant, you are not a stranger long in the West. The shell of grave formality is soon pierced, especially when the visitor is a man; and once you are through you find that the rancher and the cowboy are hearty and merry and easy in their manners. They live in a world of first names and nicknames: Jack and Smoky, Shorty and Hank. Where the older West still lingers, as it does around Wickenburg, where we have stayed, you have a pleasant glimpse of that classless society about which we hear so much now. The equality may be an illusion, but the manners do not hint at any suspicions of inferiority and superiority. To return to England, after a few months of this, is like dropping back into the feudal system.

Many Americans, usually people who have money and leisure, take to English country-house life as ducks to water, and tell us how enchanted they are by the good manners they find in this fading world of aristocratic landowners and hat-touching tenants, and how delighted they are to have left behind their native democracy of bad manners. But if they had moved West—which would have been more sensible than coming to England to play charades all day—they might have discovered there a democracy of good manners. It is made up, as all such societies will have to be, of people who are reasonably sure of themselves, easy in their own minds, not galled by feelings of inferiority, and are ready to take others as they find them. And I prefer a classless society in which you are Smoky and he is Hank and I am Jack, to one in which we are all official comrades. I would rather be Mr. Priestley first, then Jack afterwards, than Comrade Priestley all the time. In fact, I don't want to be Comrade Priestley at all.

Thinking, then, of all those Arizona people around me, fast asleep while I smoked and ruminated in my hut, I considered—not too pompously, I hope—the little classless society they had temporarily evolved. How had they achieved this appearance of happy equality? There are not many of them, of course, and they all live very close to the desert and the mountains, and might still be called pioneers. There are no great inequalities of income or privilege. If most of these people sat down to the same dinner, some would not feel they were feasting while others felt they were fasting. There are few rags, fewer diamonds. The conventional Western clothes, adapted to the climate and to the conditions of work and play, are almost like a uniform, in spite of the cowboy's native dandyism; and this helps, too.

I sorted out these reasons not because I had any pretensions to be a social analyst of Western life, not because of any interest I had in that part of the world, but because the general problem seemed important. I had read and heard a good deal about it. We are always being offered systems of reform or revolution that will promptly remove all inequalities. The Communists talk to us about their classless society. We must remember, though, that they are thinking in terms of the Marxian dialectic and are referring to a world seen as a highly simplified economic structure. But obviously there can still be classes, and with them all the bitterness of inequality, even when the means of production have passed into the keeping of the state. In Russia, I gather, there is as yet no pretense of real equality. The old class distinctions have gone, but a new set, even more ironbound, has taken their place. Because the Party official, occupying an important position, is not paid any more than most people, that does not prove he is no better off than they are; he may be given a number of pleasant things that would have to be bought and paid for in other countries. I have heard Bernard Shaw argue eloquently against the smallest inequalities in income, and demonstrate that anything short of a genuine equality of pay all around will keep us entangled in this sticky web of money, and poison all our relations with one another. But Shaw appears to believe in privilege. And this will not do. He has never lived in a society in which money did not mean much but privilege meant a great deal. And I have. I served over four and a half years in the army, where money does not count for much and privilege, carefully adjusted according to rank and then very strongly enforced, counts for a lot. A wealthy private soldier is not allowed to be insolent to a poor officer. Money might bribe a little promotion, but that is all. Whereas there is a tremendous difference between what a private soldier is allowed to do and what a general is allowed to do. And to my mind this is far more galling than any difference of income, provided that that difference is above a certain level. Once the low level is raised, from starvation to decent comfort, the inequalities do not seem to me to matter very much. Henry Ford and the Duke of Westminster have more money than I can ever hope to have, but as I am not poor myself, have not to wonder where the next meal is coming from, I have never wasted a single second envying either of them.

This does not mean that I cannot see that an immensely rich man may have far more power than any private person in a so-called democracy has any right to possess, just as if he owned an army or navy of his own. But that is a different argument, belonging to politics and economics. What I maintain is that as soon as everybody has a little more than enough to live on decently, we should be better off with what inequalities of income there may be left than we should be with equal incomes under a system of state privilege, organized with military precision. Thus—to take a small example—most seats at the opera are expensive, and it may be said that as conditions are now in America or

England, attendance at the opera is one of the privileges of the rich. Smith has a passion for opera and is not rich. What can he do? The answer is that it is hard luck, but that it might be worse, for at least he can save enough to buy an occasional seat. But under an equal-income-and-state-privilege system, though opera seats might cost nothing at all, they also might be strictly allotted as perquisites to members of one or two privileged classes, and if Smith—who may be always out of luck—did not happen to belong to those classes, he would never get near the opera. In England during the war, when Smith was a private soldier, he was never allowed, when in uniform, to enter the more comfortable rooms in many taverns. Now that he is out of uniform, he can at least decide for himself whether the extra comfort is worth the extra penny or so he will have to pay for his drink in the better room.

In short, equal income severely tempered by privilege would not enlarge, but further restrict, the liberty of the individual. What is needed is a juster distribution of wealth with as little privilege as possible. Owing to certain local and temporary conditions, a state like Arizona comes nearer to achieving this than the older communities do, with the result that it seems far nearer to our idea of a free and happy democracy.

Chapter Seven

THERE was a time not very long ago when these ranches in northern Arizona carried feed for vast herds of cattle. But what the cattle left, the sheep that followed almost completely destroyed, pulling up the very roots. The goose with the golden eggs was cooked for one fine merry meal. And I gather that there has been during these last fifty years in America a great killing and cooking of these golden-egged geese. The rugged individuals of one generation have bequeathed to their sons little more than an opportunity to be ruggeder still. The desert hills have been swept clean of feed for cattle; forests containing easily marketable timber have been massacred without quarter; mines have been worked in what once seemed the cheapest way, but in what has since proved to be the most expensive fashion; and the mottoes have been *A short life but a gay one* and *Here today, gone tomorrow*.

The economist's knowledge and sharp eye for facts are not mine; I cannot pretend to any better observation than what is usual in a wandering man of letters; yet even I have been struck by the fact that these states have had an economic past, that there are signs of departed yesterdays as well as of glorious tomorrows.

We Europeans are taught to think of the United States as the country that is only just beginning, the land of unlimited opportunity, the place that is all a golden future. What we see in New York only confirms this belief. Here are people who with an astonishing ease and confidence seem to rebuild their magnificent city every few years. Buildings that our own cities would be glad to boast about are torn down, as if they were nothing better than a huddle of slums, and new towers and palaces go shooting up, glorious in that clear light. We are not merely impressed, we are almost terrified. We are pygmies watching the giants at play. If this is what is happening in the greatest American city, then, in spite of certain disturbing rumors, the whole vast land must be dripping with milk and honey, the cleanest certificated milk, the sweetest and most nutritious honey. We might as well all move across, to enjoy this superb plumbing, these phenomenally cheap automobiles, these hygienically-sealed packages of food, the whole bewildering bounty of this continent and its new civilization, and let Europe dwindle into a tourists' playground, inhabited by guides and head waiters. There are not a hundred and fifty millions living here yet. Absurd! Make it three, four, five hundred millions. Let the whole world begin again here, dating the new era of plenty from the Declaration of Independence.

Then the dream is shattered. Even after we have traveled among these states and have been surprised by what we have seen, we may still believe—as I still believe—that the United States, with its huge resources and its undiminished stores of energy and enterprise, is the Land of the future, with the Soviet Union, binding half Asia to itself, as the only possible rival. But we realize that the epic of this land will not be the economic fairy tale of our imagination. No manna will descend from the skies. We are astonished to find in a country that is still so new so many witnesses to enterprises already dead and gone. The trains that carry us from one growing city to another take us past farmsteads that seem neglected, forlorn, ruined. In the West, we hear tales of ranching that are now as far in the past as the tale of Sheridan's ride. We can visit, as I have done, whole ghostly chains of dead mining-towns, with their own deserted railway tracks, stations, sidings, hotels.

There is probably no region in America newer and more proudly flourishing than that of southern California, which supplies our motorcars with gasoline, our dining-tables with orange juice, and our picture theaters with films. In the modern world, we may say that southern California is "sitting pretty." One reason why people like to live down there is that the sun shines nearly every day and it hardly ever rains. Unfortunately, millions of people, with their houses and factories and fruit farms, need a great deal of rain; and so the ghost of drought haunts this region. It has room for millions more, but will it have water for them?

What will happen if the population steadily increases and there come a few unusually dry years? We are told that Boulder Dam has been built to regulate the supply of water into Imperial Valley and to sell the coast towns cheap electric power. But I suspect that all the people in those towns are glad to know that behind that vast wall in the mountains is a great new lake of fresh water.

We had seen Boulder Dam, and had pointed our ciné-kodak at it so that we could see a moving shadow of its splendor when we returned home. In order to see it, we traveled for hours and hours along narrow dirt roads through the high emptiness of Nevada. Anybody who is under the impression that the world is becoming too crowded should move into Nevada. If the whole of Great Britain were inhabited by the people of Oxford, there would still be more folk about than there are in Nevada. A road there seems to lead endlessly from nothing to nothing. A solitary filling station soon gives the Nevada traveler a sense of a bustling urban life. When they do achieve a town there, they throw it wide open, probably feeling that any restriction would be intolerable at the end of such trails. Reno, with its divorcing, and Las Vegas, with its all-night gambling, are tiny oases in an immense mile-high desert. To meet a few other human beings in Nevada is to assist at a miracle. Here, like the young Mark Twain, they are roughing it still. Anything new that has been introduced since his time is lost in these vacant immensities.

Except Boulder Dam. And that is worth traveling weeks to see. It is like the beginning of a new world, that world we catch a glimpse of in one of the later sequences of Wells' film, "Things to Come," a world of giant machines and titanic communal enterprises. Here in this Western American wilderness, the new man, the man of the future, has done something, and what he has done takes your breath away. When you look down at that vast smooth wall, at its towers of concrete, its power stations, at the new lakes and cataracts it has created; and you see the men who have made it all moving far below like ants or swinging perilously in midair as if they were little spiders; and you note the majestic order and rhythm of the work—you are visited by emotions that are hard to describe, if only because some of them are as new as the great dam itself.

Compared with this piece of building, the recent skyscrapers seem like toys. The shining towers of New York merely express the new man in his initial playful mood. With Boulder Dam he has really set to work. This is what he can do when given a real job. This is a first glimpse of what chemistry and mathematics and engineering and large-scale organization can accomplish when collective planning unites and inspires them. Here is the soul of America under socialism. This is the reply to the old heedless, wasteful individualism.

Some Americans I met grumbled to me about the cost of the dam, and dropped the usual hints about nest-feathering. I was a visitor and it was not for me to tell them they were wrong, even though I have the privilege of paying American taxes myself while not being granted any other privilege of the ordinary American citizen. But if any of the dollars taken from me went towards paying the cost of Boulder Dam, I am more than satisfied, I am proud and delighted. The Colorado River must not be allowed to do what it likes. Imperial Valley cannot exist in constant danger of flood or drought. The electric power that is carried over the hundreds of miles of desert to the coast will light up the faces of Chaplin and Garbo for us. There may come a season soon when all the water in Boulder Canyon will be urgently needed.

So much for utility. But Boulder Dam is something more than a vast utilitarian device, a super-gadget. Enchanted by its clean functional lines and at the same time awed by its colossal size, you might be tempted to call it a work of art; as if something that began with utility and civil engineering ended somewhere in the neighborhood of Beethoven's "Ninth Symphony." There is no doubt whatever that it is a thing of beauty, and that the impression it makes on any sensitive observer is not unlike that made by a massive work of art. But if you feel that language is being abused here, and hold that nothing so impersonal as a dam can be a genuine work of art, then you have to find some new way of accurately describing this new creation.

It remains in my memory, an inspiring image, as a kind of giant symbol. It is the symbol of the new man, a new world, a new way of life. In this new world, men who know and care nothing about art, who might foolishly despise artists, can be driven by sheer necessity to gigantic collective action, and through that action can produce something that is at once stupendous and impersonally beautiful. We see these new men at work everywhere. It is they who design and build our modern vehicles, our cars and engines, airplanes and ships. Everything they do is impersonal. They do not sign their names and talk about their temperaments. We do not know who they are. But their creations are everywhere, and even when such creations are engines of death, as they so frequently are in this sad muddle we are in, they do not fail to satisfy or sometimes to exhilarate us. It is probably true to say that in these days our æsthetic emotions are more often stirred outside the narrow circles of art than inside them. The nameless men move us when the artists have failed.

It is possible that we shall soon have to give up many things dear to us. Time hath a wallet on his back. A great deal of deck cargo may have to be thrown overboard in order to save the ship. The adolescent frolics of individualism must give way to the sober adult task of coöperation. Already, much that was admirable in its day has gone or is going. Even at my age I know there is much to regret, and when I am feeling less than my age, and more than my age, in short, am feeling at once senile and childish, I find myself cursing this relentless movement of the time spirit. Like most writers, I delight in what is individual to the point of eccentricity, in the whimsical and freakish, in characters that are magnificently themselves; and I welcome real persons and distrust crowds and mass movements. I take little pleasure in what is new and slick and standardized, preferring what is old and crabbed and richly individual. Not being of a mechanical turn of mind, I am suspicious and rather frightened of machinery. The sight of any highly mechanized and super-efficient process chills rather than warms my heart. I do not like the way in which we think of humanity increasingly in terms of abstractions of it, turning real people into consumers, operatives, customers, passengers, and the rest. I am both irritated and alarmed by the emergence of States and Parties that are considered to be more important than the sum total of the persons they should be serving. I believe that ordinary human happiness is the great thing, and that somehow we are now creating all kinds of monsters— the State, the Party, Industrial Efficiency—to whom ordinary human happiness is nothing. Sometimes in my despair I feel that, short of being a slave, a serf, a miserable peasant, I could have been happier in any other age.

Then I have the sense and decency to remember that there have always been a great many slaves, serfs, miserable peasants, poor bewildered wretches toiling from dark to dark that a few of their betters should have warmth and light; and to tell myself that vaguely sentimentalizing over a favored group (whose dirt and disease and narrow outlook we are apt to forget) is not entertaining a true vision of the past. The world is as it is, with our social consciences as part of it, and no occasional bouts of self-pity will push the world back or stop those consciences working. And then I see that we have to scrap many things we hold dear to keep the rest secure. I may like persons and distrust mass movements, but we may be in such a dangerous situation that there must be mass movements in order to save persons.

The world that will emerge, that is already emerging, though not yet secure, may be strange and uncomfortable to us. Old landmarks will be missing. A certain cozy individuality may have vanished forever. Many things will be new and coldly indifferent. Yet now and then I feel that I am catching a glimpse of this new world that is more reassuring than my own vague anticipation of it, probably because it is easier to imagine what will be missing from it than it is to fill this world with new splendors of its own.

And Boulder Dam, that vast impersonal work of utility-art, that expression of new collective humanity, remains in my memory as one of those reassuring glimpses. Perhaps we shall soon say good-by forever to the *magic casements, opening on the foam of perilous seas, in faery lands forlorn.* Perhaps the words will lose their enchantment; the images they call up will seem idle or evil; and the author of them, if remembered, will seem a fretting, childish dreamer. But if this worst should happen, and the magic casements open no more and the poets and the painters be all silent and still, I take some comfort from the thought that I can stand with the crowd, nameless humanity at ease watching nameless humanity at work, and be filled with wonder and awe as new Boulder Dams arise.

Chapter Eight

AT THIS point in my revery in front of the stove, with midnight round me, I forgot both myself and the places and things I had seen that winter, and began considering, with no great precision, political America. For I saw then the astonishing contrast between American life and its political thinking. We are told over and over again that the American is strongly individualist. Every day, at least one newspaper repeated with pride the statement that America is the stronghold of individualism, and most of the leader-writers did not hesitate to put in front the good old "rugged."

America has always had its individualism, and always will have. That is what is said, and it appears to be generally believed. Even the political opponents of individualism, members of the various collectivist groups, mostly denounce it without questioning its reality. They accept it as one of the great evil realities. And everybody else might be said to nail it to the Constitution. Roosevelt's government might act at times as if it really believed in socialism, but it is recognized that these are temporary measures, due to the urgency of the times, and that any lapse from pure individualism is merely like the lapse from good manners of a host who has to tell a drunken guest to clear out. The ordinary American appears to be far more frightened of names than he is of measures. So long as he is repeatedly told that his individualism remains inviolate, he can be persuaded to welcome schemes that look to an outsider quite boldly socialistic. Call him a "Red" or even a "Radical" and he may want to knock you down. This is because the popular press has told him over and over again that Radicals and Reds are immoral, cranky, dirty ruffians, the opposite of "regular fellows." And the ordinary American citizen does not want to be odd, critical, detached, whimsical, rebellious; he wants to be solidly fixed into the community, a regular fellow. In short, his outlook is not strongly individualistic, and when he denounces the Reds and Radicals for wanting to rob him of his individualism, it is really their own individualism that is irritating him.

Again, I had long been puzzled by one peculiar fact. I could not understand why Bolshevik Russia, which dislikes individualism in every form, should have long regarded the United States with admiration, to the extent of most flattering imitation. The good Russian citizen is asked to observe and imitate the still better American citizen. It is true that Russia wishes to industrialize herself, and that large-scale industry is superbly organized and efficient in America. That explains some of this admiration and imitation, but not all. Thus, there are many things that the Russian does badly that are superbly done in France, but the ordinary French citizen does not serve as a model in Moscow. Why not? Because, I suggest, Stalin and his friends, who are very acute, know that there is something fundamentally hostile to the communal and collectivist ideal in the French, whereas in America, notwithstanding her intrenched capitalism and her boast of being so strongly individualistic, there is not this fundamental hostility, that in America the battle is already half won. American economists and politicians and newspaper editors may go on and on shouting about their individualism, but the great unconscious drift of American life, it seemed to me, was away from it, set towards a very different shore.

It is one of the notable weaknesses of our time that the tremendous scale of things compels us to specialize. Thus, the economist dare not travel far from his economics. There are always masses of statistics waiting for him. On the other hand, a writer like myself, who is primarily interested in people and social life and the arts, cannot pretend to argue on level terms about their own subjects with the political and economic specialists. The result is that all the time we are given cross-sections instead of wholes. The great synthesis cannot be attempted. I had read, this winter, John Strachey's *The Coming Struggle for Power*, and felt in agreement with much of it. But in the middle of his argument, Strachey, with laudable courage, tries to give us a sample of Communist literary criticism, offering his own account of such writers as Proust, Lawrence, Aldous Huxley, all subtle, confused, bewildering personalities. The result was horribly superficial and misleading. Only the feeblest ray of light was directed into the fascinating deep gloom of these minds. Thus, a whole section of an honest and courageous book seemed trivial, almost contemptible. And that is what happens to us now when we try to enlarge our bounds.

On the other hand, it is important that the great topics of our time should be approached from as many different directions as possible; they must be thoroughly besieged. So I did not consider that I was wasting my own time, with some danger afterwards of wasting my readers' time, when I began to examine this problem of American individualism in the light of what I had almost casually observed about American life in my own travels. I realized at once that what had always impressed me in America had never seemed to belong to a strongly individualistic civilization. On the contrary, it was not by what a single person can accomplish, but always by what can be done by collective effort that America had always shown herself so new, formidable, and fascinating. Such arts as poetry and painting and sculpture and the subtler forms of musical composition and execution, these were individual, and America could not pretend to excel in any of them. Architecture is far less individual, depends far more upon coöperation, and

[119]

America had evolved an immense new architecture of her own. On the same high level of achievement were her triumphs of civil engineering. The American theater was not inferior to the various contemporary European theaters, but it had depended for its success not on outstanding personalities but on very energetic and conscientious team work. (Like American football, which differs from the English in its substitution of intricate mass play for individual initiative.) We know that films do not readily lend themselves to the expression of individuality, that they demand an immense collaboration, and that even where they would be better with fewer hands and heads at work on them—as, for example, in the scenarios—they are very much the joint production. And we know that it is in the manufacture of films that America has easily excelled. There are a few films that express an individuality. The more recent Chaplin films, acted, written, directed, composed by Chaplin, are perhaps the best of these exceptions. But Chaplin is not American, but English. Even after all these years in America, his outlook is still European. And it is the Europeans in Hollywood who have most trouble with the film organizations that employ them, who are always trying to express themselves, refusing to be a cog in the magnificent machine.

It has been my experience in America, as a visitor who has occasionally to do some shopping, that the article that one man can make is usually a worse job than the European one, but that the things that can only be manufactured by an elaborate collective effort—such as automobiles—are better and cheaper than those in Europe. It is also significant that American factory methods have traveled farther from the old individualism of the craftsman than factory methods in England, Germany, France, and have done so triumphantly, the cheers drowning the few protests. What used to be regarded as one of the chief weaknesses of the collectivist state—its probable strong tendency towards standardization—has been hard at work remolding American social life these last two generations.

The collective man, the socialist citizen, is not a weird new type that may arrive in the United States any year now. In almost all but his theories, the average modern American *is* the collective man. His impulsive advances seem to be always away from that famous individualism. He has no objection to mass movement. Nearly everything he does is being done about the same time by a million others. He likes doing exactly what all the others are doing. So does his wife. That is why America is the country of awful flops and sudden gigantic successes; fifty books will lie down and quietly die, while the fifty-first will sell by the hundred thousand, go raging through the land like a plague. One winter when I was over here, half the people in every state I visited seemed to stop their work and play every night to listen to Amos and Andy on the radio; in the drug stores and hotel lobbies of small towns, if there was a public radio, people crowded in, then instantly froze, to listen; but the very next time I came here, though the two comedians were still on the radio, nobody seemed to bother about them much. No doubt they were still popular, but the vast Amos and Andy fever had subsided. People in other countries suddenly adopt favorites and then drop them, but not, I think, with the same astonishing unanimity. The nation-wide craze—for a book, a comedian, a game, a diet—is very American; and not because the Americans have less sense and more hysteria than other people, but because they are more anxious to be regular fellows, to enjoy what everybody is enjoying, and not to appear oddly different, superior, cranky, eccentric, too individualistic.

I know that there are good historical reasons for this tendency towards standardization. America for generations was faced with the task of turning hordes of immigrants into good American citizens, and it had to be done quickly. Therefore the social emphasis had to be upon likeness. The greatest civil war this world has yet seen was fought in these states so that not only political unity, but also one kind of civilization, could be enforced on them all. The Bolshevik leaders have had the task of turning Russians into good Communist citizens, and they too have had to work quickly. Therefore, they have, perhaps instinctively, looked towards America, and have carefully turned away from the older and more genuinely individualistic countries. They have been inspired by something more than American factory methods. They have recognized across the ocean that separates these two great land-masses a people who, while saluting the old banners of economic individualism, are always busy expressing themselves collectively, and doing it with an ease, force, and natural cohesion beyond Lenin's dreams.

The difference is, of course, that the Russian plan for their society is all of a piece. Theory and practice are one; which is the strength of Communism. In America, popular political and economic theory go one way, while the great drift of social tendencies goes in the opposite direction. This may be one explanation of the queer nervous stress of American life. Such a vast contradiction can start innumerable deep conflicts, tearing good minds in two. Having arrived at this point, I remembered then various American novels I had recently read, sincere and urgent fiction even if not works of genius, and recollected how I had been impressed, time after time, with this sense of stress, of some hidden strain that had nothing to do with sex and money, of bewildered sad characters who felt isolated, almost outlawed, and did not know why. And then Thomas Wolfe came into my mind, perhaps because I had read, not long before, his *Time And The River*. A young man with many obvious faults, apparently including a lack of invention, but undoubtedly one of the rare big chaps, a sort of giant, one of those great sprawling writers whose work you can easily correct but whose virtues lie beyond your pains. In his Mississippies of dithyrambic prose, Wolfe is expressing his country in this age, putting it all in as fast as he can; and remembering the effect his two big novels had on me, I saw that not all the neat propaganda jobs issued by the Soviet Department of Fiction had given me such a deep sense of community, of people in the mass, of humanity stretched anonymously across plains and mountains, as the very American Wolfe had done. And I saw behind him the shadow of Whitman, the poet of nameless comrades, of whole crowds of plain folk, who obliterated individuality in both his subjects and his style, who could easily have been the chosen poet of a new collectivist state, singing to Russians not yet born.

What then, I asked myself, was my conclusion, stated plainly, without any kindly blur of metaphor. Surely it was this. That the economic and political framework of America, even when twisted out of its old shape by the New Deal, was wrong. It no longer fitted the deep instinctive life of the people. What seemed to me new, valuable, vital, satisfying, grandly expressive of the national character, no longer appeared to belong to an individualistic habit of mind, but had been produced by collective action, inspired by deeply communal feeling. American life was not being enlarged and enriched by a comparative few gifted and creative individuals, but by huge impersonal creative forces working through the whole community. The politicians and the professors and the big business men were really far behind the times, were anachronisms when compared with the men with the blue prints and the blue jeans. Practice was pouring out millions of razor blades, while theory was still wearing long whiskers. The New Deal, which at least had some glimmer of a notion of social justice and did not see the life of the community as a kind of dog fight, was better than the bad old deal, but it was far from being good enough. It was still old-fashioned politics, belonging to the world of the court house and the levee, not to the world of the Empire State Building and Boulder Dam.

What, then, was needed? Dictatorship by the young Marxists I had met in New York? No, that did not necessarily follow. First, I thought, this old story of America's individualism should be brought to an end. It no longer shows us the best of America, but the worst. It is the striped and star-spangled cloak of the surviving buccaneers. It is as much out-of-date as the old admiration of men who merely happened to be more predatory and unscrupulous than their neighbors, those millionaires now pilloried in book after book. Then, I thought, the native genius of these people for large-scale organization, for concerted effort, for tremendous team work, must be allowed to find expression in fitting political and economic forms. This meant some kind of collec-

tivist state, an ultimate socialism. It does not follow—
and it is the weakness of most Communists that they
cannot see that this does not follow—that the Russian
experiment must be imitated, with success or failure
along the line Marx-Lenin-Stalin. It might well be
that there cannot be found in any existing theoretical
work the vaguest outline of the socialism that could be
ultimately achieved in America. For I believed that the
American could solve his political and economic problems as he has so triumphantly solved his architectural
and engineering problems—magnificently in his own
way. But that did not shake my conviction that that way
must sooner or later lead him to some form of socialism.

This was all very fine, with nobody but my midnight
self to argue with, but when I remembered my fellow
guests on the ranch, I felt some misgiving. They were
pleasant, friendly people, not rich, perhaps, but all
comfortably situated, who had come here from New
York, Boston, New Jersey, Chicago, Kansas City, to
recuperate themselves, to bring out a delicate child, or
to dodge a nervous breakdown. I had enjoyed playing
tennis and bridge with them, and they were indulgent
enough with me; but I could imagine, after our odd
moments of political talk, the look they would give me
if they learned I had sat up in my little hut and coolly
handed them all over to socialism. They had, I guessed,
very definite opinions about socialism. They saw it as a
colossal racket, run by a lot of bloodthirsty, dirty,

foreign-born ruffians, far lower down the human scale than the underworld rats of the Prohibition era. One or two of them, perhaps, might not take such a melodramatic view, but even they would assume that under socialism the people would be robbed all the time. They were mostly Republicans, and so they regarded the Democrats with marked disfavor, as a cunning, tub-thumping, unscrupulous gang of demagogues. But the worst Democrat, the most ferocious New Dealer, was still a fellow citizen, who could possibly be argued with, a real American and not some scarlet alien monster, or, alternatively, some wretched driveling lunatic. Some of them talked a good deal about politics, but they were politics of the peculiarly American kind, nearly as local and about as philosophical as the affairs of a baseball league. To a stranger, American politics seem the oddest in the world, for he finds it almost impossible to discover in them any of the usual backgrounds of temperament and general theory. They remind him of some violent and involved family quarrel. He begins to feel that somewhere or other, beyond the arena of these meaningless conflicts, there must be real politics going on. But he only finds them in a few groups and books. All the newspapers seem to be busy in the two-ring circus.

My fellow guests, of course, would take the opposite view. They would see socialism as something outside real politics, as little to do with the great realities of American political life as Menuhin's performance of the Brahms Violin Concerto. But among those realities, to be deplored but apparently not to be changed, was the good old spoils system, which hopefully appointed good party men to be public servants. I had heard more and more criticism of this system, for, now that taxes were no longer light and government expenditure was reaching astronomical figures, it was beginning to be realized that a fine, big-hearted party man might not always be the best person to administer public funds. I had also heard many complimentary remarks on the English system, which the speakers seemed to imagine had existed for centuries and was probably based on some sort of aristocratic English integrity. They did not know that in the old and very aristocratic days there had been any amount of corruption, and that the present system only dates from 1870, when Gladstone threw the civil services open to competition. I remembered that the one or two of them who were in favor of changing this party patronage system of running the country, seemed to me to imagine that the change would take generations, whereas I believe that, forcefully backed by public opinion, the change could be complete within a few years. At first, perhaps, a good many fine big-hearted creatures might have to be taken to jail and be given thumping big sentences of imprisonment. The others would soon learn. And careful honest men, of a type already employed in many federal departments, could easily be found to take the places of these dashing political fellows, for America has its share of them. It is merely that the tradition is against them.

I remembered how shocked I had been to hear two American attorneys, themselves honest professional men, discussing a certain official in charge of a state project, and observing casually that such a man, with his four or five thousand dollars a year of salary and doubtful prospects, could not be blamed, of course, for feathering his own nest. Clearly, in their view you could not buy honesty in a public official at such a price. No doubt that was true, and would always be true, while there was a genial tradition of dishonesty, which men who were honest themselves did not even condemn. It is this tradition that makes it possible in America to buy things that ought not to be for sale. Rich corporations buy the law; advertisers buy men of science; criminals buy the police force; employers buy slugging fists and machine-guns to protect their greed. England, of course, has its own tradition of corruption, not so crude and raw. It is no use offering money to officials there, but social influence and the promise of privilege will do a great deal. Both traditions are bad, and both could be smashed to smithereens in a few years by a people who suddenly lost patience. But—oh—the long, dumb patience of the people! They need all the poets to speak for them:

*Smile at us, pay us, pass us; but do not quite
    forget;
For we are the people of England, that never
    have spoken yet.*

And the people of America, so vast and confused, often still stumbling between what remains of an old language and the beginning of a new, have not spoken yet.

Once they have broken this bad old tradition—and already the great unconscious drift towards collectivism in America eddies around it like the Mississippi in flood encircling some old shanty—these American acquaintances would be better citizens of a socialist state, I concluded, than I would myself. There are many possible features of such a state that I would deeply resent and that they would cheerfully accept. They did not seem to me to have any strong desire for that liberty which allows individual experiment in living. They welcomed authoritative guidance on all matters, were always looking for it. Their women were always richly rewarding anybody who turned up to bully them into some sort of Utopian conformity. The men followed on, grinning and grumbling a little at times, but not rebelling. If they were in the service of colossal commercial concerns, they accepted with docility, perhaps with downright gratitude, arbitrary and inquisitorial methods that would have seemed to me intolerable. The persecution of odd minorities never appeared to arouse their indignation: oddity seemed to them a worse crime than tyrannical suppression. And I felt that if most of them had been suddenly transported to one of the totalitarian states, they would have noticed the lack of comfort long before they would have noticed the loss of liberty.

What about Fascism then? Would it be possible, if very astutely worked, to conjure some stars-and-stripes form of Fascism on them? Had the average American ever very strongly objected to what is typical of Fascism: the suppression by force of industrial revolt; the relentless gagging of critical minorities; government on gangster lines; highly organized and ceaseless propaganda; a pseudo-mystical nationalism, with some pseudoscience thrown in, all calculated to arouse the maximum of mass emotion? Perhaps not. Yet there was something about these states beyond their mere size that seemed to me deeply hostile to the Fascist idea, except in so far as it represented the sense of community, something that did not recoil from violence, but was definitely unmilitary, knew no tradition of fear of bordering powers, and was not wistful of old-fashioned drum-and-trumpet glory. The pioneer who lingers in the American character is not good Fascist material. It may be objected that he is not good socialist material. About that, I am less certain. The pioneer was intensely, jealously democratic; he was less a solitary adventurer than

the advance guard of community; he saw the commonwealth come into being, and frequently at some stage
of his life he sacrificed part of his liberty to give that
commonwealth order and law. And just as the new
America shows us the result of huge impersonal creative
forces working through the whole community, so, oddly
enough, the older America was nearly always chosen as
the scene of early communal experiments in living, both
religious and secular. In short, it seemed to me that they
were all in their nature—though not in their immediate
political theory—closer to socialist citizenship than I
was myself.

A belief in some form of socialism—and the form has
often changed—is not with me, as it is with many persons, an act of rebellion, but almost something belonging
to tradition and filial piety. I was brought up among
socialists, not the embittered rebels of today, but the
gentle, hopeful theorists of thirty or forty years ago.
My father, who was both a better and happier man than
I am, was a socialist; and there was nothing odd about
that, for the industrial town where he and I were born
had strong radical and labor sympathies. (The old
workingpeople could remember being sent off to the factories in the dark, shivering and half asleep, and staying there, among the machines, until it was dark again
—and they were little more than babies. A great many
important, public-spirited gentlemen stoutly opposed
any attempt to keep these small children out of the

mills, on the ground that any interference would ruin the wool and cotton trades. The children were taken out, and the wool and cotton trades survived their disappearance. That was long ago. But the same sort of people are talking the same miserable twaddle today.) My father was a schoolmaster, and a very good one, with an almost ludicrous passion for acquiring and imparting knowledge. He was not a born scholar, but he was a born teacher. Outside his school he did a great deal of useful public service—speaking, helping to organize, working on committees, and so on—not because he was a busybody or was socially ambitious, but because he was essentially public-spirited, the type of citizen that democratic theorists have in mind but rarely in actual view. But there was nothing of the smooth committee humbug about him. He was very brisk, humorous, stout-hearted, not to be patronized or bullied. I am commonly supposed to be pugnacious, but he was at heart ten times more pugnacious than I am, and if you went one step too far with him, his ruddy face turned scarlet, his eyes were electric blue, and he came roaring at you like a little lion.

He had the only sensible way of dealing with money, and I am glad to say that he bequeathed it to me. This is to realize as soon as possible what kind of life you can lead with the money at your disposal (and he had never much, yet was never dissatisfied), then within that circle to live at your ease, never worrying about money.

He deliberately shut out one sort of life—the more expensive life of hotels, restaurants, cabs, theater stalls, Havana cigars, liqueur brandies—and then lived like a king in the dominions left to him. To think hard and realistically about money, then to forget it, that is what neither spendthrifts nor misers can do, and it is the only way to be merry and wise. He was not a romantic figure, did not pretend to be. His world lacked glitter and glamor. I never remember seeing him either in ecstasies or yet defeated by despair. But he never failed a duty, left the world better than he found it, was loved by his friends and respected by his army of acquaintances, and had a lot of fun. Beneath the rather droll surface peculiarities—his love of making acquaintances, of asking questions, of imparting information; his fear of minor social criticism; his distrust of the picturesque, romantic, grandiose things of this life; his odd mixture of patience and explosive hot temper—he was a living rock of good solid human nature. If I was picking a team to go and colonize another planet, I would choose his kind first.

Years ago, when my first scribblings were achieving print, he was proud of me; and now, too long after we exchanged our last words, I think I am prouder still of him. Because he did not want too much himself and hated to see others have too little, because he knew that life now has something better to offer than a universal all-in wrestling match for money, because he knew that there were more and more people like himself coming into the world, people who could be trusted to do their duty by the public that employed him, who did not need to be threatened with starvation nor inspired by greed, he believed not only in government for the people by the people, but also in production, which touches us more than government does, by the people for the people, and so was a socialist. And he remains in my memory as the ideal socialist citizen. Of such could be made the best kingdom yet on this earth.

It occurred to me then that my father could have tolerated or even enjoyed, just as many of the Americans I knew could tolerate and even enjoy, many features of a collectivist state that I should myself dislike. There was more wilful individualism in me than in him, or in them. I set more store by independent lines of thought and by individual experiments in living than he did or they do. This much I knew. But, I asked myself, what kind of socialist state had I in mind? I remembered then one of a series of wireless talks I had given in London, some years before. In these talks I had been allowed to discuss anything and everything, within the limits of the rather puritanical censorship of our B.B.C., and in this particular talk I had gayly outlined my perfect state. And, though consistency is not one of my virtues or vices, I did not think I had changed much since then. What had I said? I remembered, after a struggle, that I had begun by declaring that in my

[135]

country—and I could imagine how ten thousand furious old gentlemen switched off their wireless sets at this very point—nobody works for a living. I meant for a bare living, and probably said so. The whole talk was coming back to me now. I could bring its argument into the present tense. In my country, then, nobody works for a bare living. The state owns all the vital necessaries of life, and distributes them gratis. Nor do I believe there is anything crazy in this. You work there for luxuries and privileges, and if you want luxuries and privileges, as most of us do passionately, then you must work. There is no having it both ways in my country, no grabbing all the luxuries and privileges, and not even working for them. And by necessaries, we mean necessaries; clean shelter, plain food, some clothing, and not drinks and cigarettes and money for gambling and visits to the films. And I do not think many people would prefer not to work if they were compelled to be so austere in their idleness. But there are a few—and why shouldn't there be?—who would rather live this spare life than work, odd fish like philosophers without pupils or readers, poets in the dumb stage, or born tramps, and sometimes some very remarkable folk come out of this class, and why should we dragoon them out of existence? The rest of us would have to keep them, but they would be no great charge on us, and we keep most of them now, along with a great many more expensive parasites.

[136]

But in my country we do not consider there is something mystically right and beautiful about work, not, that is, the general coöperative labor for the community. About our own private work, the thing we choose to do for ourselves, we have other and different views. And we make an important distinction, completely lost in your world, between necessaries and luxuries, what is urgently needed to maintain life and what makes it more fun, though of course there are borderline things, about which we have frequent arguments. But the point is that all necessaries are produced by the state itself, which decided that it could not have individuals claiming possession of such vital things; whereas most luxuries are produced by private enterprise. It is the difference between water and wine. The state naturally owns and distributes the water supply, but private persons, who take more interest in such matters, sell you a bottle of wine. Or bread and cake. There is a standard government bread—pleasant, wholesome, unexciting stuff—of which everyone has a share; but we do not want government cake, for cake is a matter of personal taste and personal service, so you can still buy cake, real home-made cake, in little shops. We still have money, because it is more convenient than a system of rations and credits, but of course it plays a much smaller part in the life of the community. It is more like boys' pocket money, to be jingled and spent. You cannot hoard it very long, or treat it as a commodity and deal in it. There are no financiers, no money-jugglers, in my country, and they seem as remote to us now as medieval barons or brigands. To the people in my country it would seem just as silly for a man to be able to command great power by artful dealing in money, as it would seem to you to find a man who had made himself powerful by collecting vast piles of those colored counters and chips you use in card games. In fact, in my country money is rather like those colored counters you use in card games, except that it enables you to buy flowers, wine, silk shirts, books, pictures, or whatever you fancy. But it cannot touch the necessaries of life, and is not a source of power.

If we still have private enterprise, but no dealing in money, how do our people contrive to start their businesses? The reply is that, to begin with, these businesses, being concerned only with luxuries, are not on a big scale, because we have discovered that most luxury articles are better if produced on a small scale. Then, as all necessaries are provided by the state, wages bills are not large, especially at the beginning, when people often coöperate in the enterprise. But when some sort of credit is necessary and cannot be arranged on a friendly bartering basis, then it is furnished by the state itself, which is naturally anxious that its citizens shall have as good a time as possible and so likes to see new demands being met by new supplies. It does not work perfectly, of course—we are not in heaven—and sometimes a man with a really startlingly original idea is held up for a considerable time until he can convert people to his ideas, but meanwhile he and his dependents are not starving. We have banished forever the old fear of destitution. It has made an enormous difference. The evils that so many people said would follow, have not followed. A few odd fish are idler than they might have been before, but all the others seem to be much keener and more energetic simply because they have been released from the bondage of this fear. They do not care less about things, they care a great deal more. They are gayer and more self-confident. We have released great stores of energy that could not escape before from the dreadful circles of worry. And these people freed from fear are not only much more useful than they were before; they are also much pleasanter to one another. A lot of cruelty has its origin in fear. A man feels he is being bullied by circumstance, so he begins bullying the persons in his power, and so it goes on. We have done with most of that.

But because the state, in my country, controls the production and distribution of all the necessaries of life, that does not mean that with us the state is the end of everything. On the contrary, it means that the state is merely the beginning of everything. It is the convenient arrangement that enables us to pool our resources and coöperate. It has for us no mystical significance. We do not regard it as being somehow more important than the sum total of the persons in it. By throwing the em-

phasis upon the elementary utility of the state we have
rid ourselves of all that pseudo-mystical nonsense. We
realize that it is individuals, and only individuals, who
can know joy and sorrow, not the state. If with us you
do a fine piece of work, you do it for your neighbors and
yourself, and not for the glory of the state. An arrangement that keeps the peace and supplies you with water,
bread, fuel, and light cannot be glorious. We do not
make rhetorical fervid speeches about the state, just as
nobody even in the silliest old countries talked about
donning shining armor and going out to lay down his
life for the Gas and Coke Company. Our state interferes
only in the most humdrum matters, in the bread-and-
butter departments of life. Because it is supreme here,
we see that it must be almost powerless elsewhere. Nobody wants to be told how to feel, to think, to pray, by
policemen and sanitary inspectors. You do not form an
organization to build and patrol roads, supply electricity,
bake bread, and deliver milk, and then ask it what you
ought to read. The state being with us the hewer of
wood and drawer of water, we do not allow it to be the
guardian of our private morals. If you make a public
nuisance of yourself, spoiling other people's enjoyment,
it punishes you, but it has not the impudence to pretend
to make you a better man or woman. We have given the
state a great deal of necessary business to attend to, and
we do not tolerate its interference in all that strictly
belongs to private life, in all those spheres in which

personal judgment should be supreme. So a politician with us is simply a man—or woman, for there are a great many women in this work—who is more practical than other men, a better organizer; and the old kind of politician, who was full of rhetoric, intrigue, and exhibitionism, would be useless to the prosaic, matter-of-fact state in my country, where he would probably have to go on the stage or act as a guide-lecturer to tourists.

That was all I could remember of my talk, and though it was all too easy and cheerfully cocksure, it still seemed to me to have a few grains of sound political sense gleaming in it. There was not much there that I would change. Indeed, I found myself enlarging it a little, for in that talk I had not given my system a name or explained how it might possibly come into being. Now I decided to call it Liberal Socialism. There was no doubt about its socialism, for all the more vital means of production were owned by the public, there was no longer any exploitation of one class by another class (not even of non-officials by officials, of citizens by the state, a possible form of exploitation usually overlooked by theorists of the Left), and greedy, tyrannical old capitalism was dead and buried. And because it resolutely opposed the real totalitarian state, because it acted on the belief that the individual should not be a cog in the great machine, but the reason for the machine's existence, because it drew a sharp line between what properly belongs to a communal existence and what belongs

[141]

to private life, because it denied men no right but that of enslaving other men, it was Liberal. And for a few moments, I amused myself by explaining, in terms of the now fashionable dialectic, how my Liberal Socialism had inevitably come into being. Intolerant and militant Communism had brought into existence, as antithesis, intolerant and militant Fascism, a system in which the state accepted no real economic responsibility, merely enforcing the old exploitation, but made itself supreme and ubiquitous in all other departments of life. This in turn brought into existence its opposite, the final synthesis, a system in which the state took on full economic responsibility, banishing exploitation and usury, but withdrew from all those departments of life in which the hectoring Fascist state had made itself intolerable. Thus, my Liberal Socialism. I acknowledged the generous round of applause I gave myself. While the same pipe was still alight, I had moved a long way in thought from Boulder Dam and this Far West, where I was sitting so snugly, under its wide, cold, glittering midnight. In fact, I was sitting too snugly. There was some work to do, even if it was only tidying up and destroying, and it was time I left that chair and made a beginning.

Chapter Nine

AS I began to finger the litter of letters and odd papers, dealing with it in a half-hearted fashion, I thought about our winter on this ranch. For the children, of course, it had been a season of pure happiness. They must have felt as I know I should have felt at their age if I had been suddenly packed off to join Robin Hood and Little John in Sherwood Forest. Sometimes I wondered if we had been wise to bring them here. To travel halfway round the world and go riding with cowboys, to descend into the Grand Canyon, to go on a pack trail to remote Rainbow Bridge, this is to have something to remember; but possibly it might be all too memorable, making all their travel and holiday-making for the next twenty years one long anti-climax. In short, had we given them too much all at once? I asked myself this question once more, and now suddenly decided that we hadn't. They were too young and unspoiled to spend the rest of their lives making odious comparisons. The happiness they had had in Arizona would not rob them of all possible pleasure in the Isle of Wight or Cornwall or among the Welsh mountains. They were all right. This winter would

shine in their memories, and not all their own folly or
—what was more likely—the huge dark folly of the
world, could rob them of that inner gleam.

We used to think of childhood as a sort of little anteroom to the main hall of life, an anteroom that it was
necessary to turn into a severe training-school. In this
view, the child is simply an immature adult, a little
creature on its way to real life. Childhood only lasts a
few years, is very brief compared with the possible half-
century of adult life, and therefore, it must be regarded
as a preparation for that life. I take this to be the classical view of childhood. And of course its time values, because they are so austerely objective, are all wrong.
The child's real time cannot be measured so arbitrarily.
We all remember how long the hours seemed once, and
how a single day in the country, with its tremendous
succession of adventures with buttercups and daisies and
mounds of hay, stretched out like an Oriental epic.
Nor need we discover something mystical in this, for
three months to a boy of six represent more than one-
eighteenth of his self-conscious existence, whereas three
months to a man of sixty merely pass as one-hundred-
and-eightieth of his life. And Alexis Carrel—whom I
had been reading, this winter—had suggested that as
we grow older we notice an acceleration of time because
our own inner rhythm, that of our metabolic processes,
is gradually slowing down. The other and romantic
view of childhood recognizes this difference in time

values, and remembers the immense despair, the fear and loneliness, that can blot out the sky, the vast shining territories of happiness, that the child can know, and never know again. It asks us not to treat the child as an immature adult, but as another kind of person who is eventually doomed to degenerate into what we call maturity. The poets and the romantic novelists incline to treat us as if we were all miserably exiled from childhood. The more like children we are, the better. And whether the future man or woman will be a good citizen or not, the child, the real inheritor of the earth, must be happy. Here the modern psychologists become the allies of the romantics, for they tell us that the pattern of our adult life will be laid down in our childhood, and that what warped us then will not lose its grip on us until we die. It is possible to see a good deal of human history as a record of the revenges upon the world of unhappy twisted children. The little boy who was beaten and left to sob in the dark sometimes grows up to whip whole nations and to cover great cities with darkness.

In this matter, as in so many others, I am for a compromise. The final recipe might be two-thirds romantic treatment to one-third classical. We must respect the time values of childhood, remembering that it seems to itself to exist in a huge epic life where good and evil stalk like giants. But if we persist in seeing childhood as a separate and complete state of life, an end in itself, the very children will be the first to rebuke us. For they are always pressing forward; the negotiation of every obstacle between them and maturity is a triumph; and each step out of childhood is passionately anticipated, passionately welcomed. Those of us who have young families know only too well this urge towards adult life, this blind rush onwards, and it disturbs us, frightens us. Where do they think they are going? What have we that they should throw away all that they have to join us? Parents must always have asked some such questions, but now that the world rocks and darkens every few days and peace and security seem like an old dream, often these are not queries, but cries of bitter apprehension. Yet sometimes as I watch my own children, I begin to wonder if the world as it devises new tests of courage does not perhaps create new stores of hardihood to meet them. It is not merely because they are young, ignorant, thoughtless that our children seem far less apprehensive than we are. They are more at home in this world and feel more confidence. As they grow older, they blithely accept risks that seem to us appalling. On the way to the nearest dance, they flirt not with one another but with Death. This after-the-war frontier world is breeding a race that cannot be daunted by it. My own children seem to me at once far braver and more casual than I am, or perhaps ever was. But then, I take the view that the contemporary world presses most heavily on the men of my own particular generation, that is, the men who grew up cosily in the pre-war period, spent their most impressionable years in and at the war, and have had to establish themselves as mature men, hiding all manner of scars of body and soul, in an age entirely different from that of their boyhood. We are like creatures condemned to straddle a chasm. We are the people who are forever wondering and shrinking and wincing, who have terrible dreams. Our elders were more solidly molded before 1914 and I think never quite accept the grimmer realities of the contemporary world. Our children have known nothing else, breathe its air easily, and are as gay in the lowering earthquake atmosphere as their children in their turn may be gay among the ruins. I move apprehensively about in this new age, feeling a plain coward, though I do not think I was always one. But my children hardly seem to me to realize even that their courage is ever being tested.

Even the cowboys here praised the older ones for their dashing horsemanship. All this winter we might have been a family of Tartars. The oldest pair of children have spent their days in colored shirts and scarves, blue jeans and sombreros, riding, practicing for local rodeos, and talking about riding and rodeos; the next pair, entranced tomboys, have lived an equine idyll, for when they were not riding cow ponies, they turned themselves into ponies, galloping about on all fours; and the two babies have played solemnly for hours and hours with "stick horses," taking the bits of wood out for a lope and then corralling them again in "stick horse ranch," a messy little place among the sandhills just beyond the bunk house.

Though I have gone out occasionally for an afternoon's ride, over the rough hills and then back down the dry river bed, on an enormous ruminating old animal, I had been rather out of all this, partly because I had a lot of work to do, and partly because I met the horse too late in life to find in him a satisfying companion. When he is old, sleepy, docile, he seems to me very dull; and when he is young and fresh—like the brute I had once that dashed off at full speed towards two hundred miles of waterless wilderness—he is incalculable and terrifying. I even took to going to the picnic rendezvous on the chuck-wagon, arriving there before the riders and lending a hand with the steak and potatoes and coffee. If you went to the right places among the hills, in some little lost canyon, with bluejays in the cottonwoods, or near the scarred rocks, with a million jeweled points, where you might come across an old prospector or two, baked and leathery codgers, and take a turn at the handle of the dry-washing machine, they were very good, these picnics. The sense of remoteness, the blue smoke rising in the clear aromatic air, the smell of fried steaks and coffee, the jingling of the approaching cavalcade, the whoops and yells of the cowboys, the ecstatic cries of the children; some hunger, deeper and older than that which asked for the steaks, was appeased for a little while by these things, and for an hour, the mind was at ease, the heart at rest. There is something to be said—and we in England, so certain that we are better off, rarely say it—for living in a country so spacious and sunlit that a picnic is a meal in the best dining-room. I still prefer English towns, for all their gloom, to American ones; but the American is not compelled either to stay in his town or go sloshing across wet fields. He can picnic and camp out and fish and trail-ride and loiter in forests (even listen to lectures in them, which seems all wrong) and smoke in the sunshine, and so forget many things that it is good for us sometimes to forget.

It was the first time I had seen much of American children, for the ordinary rapid traveler moves through a childless world. Perhaps those at the ranch were not typical, for either they were delicate themselves or they had one parent who was delicate. Yet I do not believe they were very different from most American children, for nobody ever suggested there was anything unusual about them. But they were unusual to me, and much stranger than their parents. Many of them were pleasant to look at, were quick and intelligent, and not without charm. But there was something very disconcerting about them. They seemed to be living at too fast a pace; they were not solid enough; they appeared to be over-excited, almost hysterical, from the moment they first got up; and they never sank quietly into themselves. Always, and not just after they had first arrived, they looked like children who had made long wearisome journeys and been kept up too late. Most of them seemed to me to be allowed to stay up far too late every night, but that is probably nothing but an English view. But there was nearly always something too bright-eyed, restless, strident, about them that suggested children at the end of a party that has gone on too long. The result was that although many of them were strong and active, they had a disturbing air of fragility. The process that would eventually turn them into quick tireless women and husky men seemed miraculous. I was always afraid that suddenly they would collapse, to lie white and shaking for weeks. But they never did. They continued giving firework displays of noise and energy, though always, it seemed, in immediate danger of bankrupting themselves. The few unpleasant ones—they were the real invalids—reminded one far more of miniature adults either drunk or crazy than of children. All of them were more adult in their tastes and style of life, though not in temperament, than our own children and others I know in England. Most of them had a tremendous precocity, sometimes amusing, sometimes alarming. To outsiders they were civil enough, but often they were very rude to their parents, who had traveled so far from the old-fashioned notion of parental authority that now they were oddly apologetic and conciliatory in their attitude towards these children, who were most exacting and shrill in their demands.

Watching some of these families—the King or Queen Child, nervous, fine-drawn, peremptory, and the anxious attendant parents—I felt at times that some procreative virtue must have left these middle-class Americans, that their fertility was on the wane, and that in consequence children were now extremely rare, coming reluctantly into the world and only surviving by a series of miracles. I had a sudden vision of that possible future described by some sociologists, a world filled with carefully preserved elderly people, in which youth would be hard to find and a baby a wonder. I know that problems of land hunger, food shortage, overcrowding, all likely to lead to war, now make us regard with some distaste the idea of teeming, spawning masses, with a birth-rate so high that the annual massacre known as infant mortality cannot keep down the population. There is too something at once messy and murderous about those people who are forever producing babies and then weeping over their coffins. We shrink from them as if they were human frogs or flies. Yet there is something healthy and heartening about an easy fat fertility, in the bouncing families we see among such races as the Italians, the Jews, the Chinese; and I for one feel uncomfortable, disturbed, when I notice the opposite tendency, a fine river of life that is rapidly dwindling into a thin uncer-

[151]

tain stream, families that consist of two anxious parents and one nervous, delicate, lordly child.

This reminded me of a half-hour I once spent in my club listening to a doctor-turned-author I knew who had just returned from a stay in the United States. In that fine careless rapture of generalization so often inspired by club sherry and a nice fire, he told me that he had come to the conclusion that there was a menacing infertile spirit hovering over these States. I cannot remember, even if he told me, whether this sterile influence came from the air, the climate, or the soil; but he was certain it existed, and that it had long rendered this country hostile to man. This explained why the Europeans who first came here did not find, as they did elsewhere, a large settled population and many signs of greater cities and empires in the past, but only a comparative handful of nomadic Indians, a pitiful number for so vast a continent. He added that the history of the old American families, the fathers and mothers of the Republic, only supported this theory. Originally, he declared, these American Anglo-Saxons were probably better stock than their cousins who stayed at home, but that they had not shown the same fertility and tenacity. The mysterious infecund bogey of these States had haunted them. He did not give me any figures, and I asked for none. It is one of my virtues as a listener that I so enjoy a massive and probably monstrous generalization for its own sake that I do not demand statistics.

Good talk would never survive the introduction of mathematical proof and a severe logic. Neither of us was unfriendly to America and its people; we did not like to think that next time we visited them there would be fewer still of the fine old Americans left; but we could not help feeling delighted at the idea of such a magnificent vampire as this, so busy keeping cradles empty, although if a St. George emerged from the Rockefeller Institute to kill it, so much the better. Probably it is all nonsense; but often when I saw these American families on the ranch, I remembered that distant half-hour in the Garrick Club.

The people I met at our own ranch and those I met from other ranches had more money than the average American citizen (though many of them were far from being rich), and some of them had worse health, but apart from these differences, they seemed typical of a stratum of American society extending over many states, ranging from New England to Alabama in one direction and to Kansas in another. Yet they often puzzled me. For example, I knew that the greater American cities have magnificent libraries and art galleries and symphony orchestras and conservatories. Yet I never heard these people talk about literature, about pictures and sculpture, about music. These things were never mentioned, though ten thousand other things were discussed. Not since I was a boy at school had I spent a winter hearing less talk about the arts. It was as if they

[153]

had ceased to exist. I could understand it if I had been living only with cowboys, although actually the cowboys have produced one or two excellent artists and have often a good ear for real music. Nevertheless, men who have spent all their lives on ranches can hardly be expected to be students of the arts. But these visitors came from some of those cities that could boast about their libraries and art galleries and concert-halls. Yet I will swear that these arts meant little or nothing to them. Then who built and filled the libraries and art galleries and concert-halls? The Jews?

There were no Jews staying on these ranches. Probably very few Jews wanted to, because the Jew, whom we prevented from owning land for centuries, has developed a strong urban tradition, and once he has left the desert does not want to spend a holiday there. But even if Jews had wished to become guests on most of these ranches, they would not have been allowed to stay. This seemed strange to me, for in England there is not a very marked anti-Semitic social prejudice. But even in England, I remembered, it was difficult to be balanced and sensible about this question. The summer before, in a series of weekly articles I had written for a newspaper, I had once tackled the subject, and had been astonished by the cataract of abusive letters that had thundered down on me. One half of them told me I ought to be ashamed of myself, a decent Anglo-Saxon, for being so pro-Jewish. The other half abused me for so clearly showing my anti-Semitic prejudices. I felt like a man who, taking a morning stroll, wanders into a pitched battle. If this was the response to one cautious little article in England, which officially has no Jewish problem, what must it be like, I wondered, in those countries that admitted to having this problem. I had noticed, as a novelist, even in England, the extreme sensitiveness of that brilliant race. One could write in a novel "He had to sit at the same table with a bony, conceited Scot" or "with a drunken, lying Irishman" or "with a brutal-headed, gruff German" or "with a common and insufferable type of Englishman," without being attacked afterwards; but if one wrote "He had to sit at the same table with a noisy, too-talkative Jew," correspondents of that race immediately enquired about one's anti-Semitic prejudice and the Jewish press sent heavily marked cuttings of very severely worded criticism. So if it would not make sense in England, it would certainly not make sense in America, where the racial problem was mixed up with all manner of fantastic social snobberies and jealousies; and I never tried to learn exactly why the very few Jews who might have wanted to winter in Arizona were not allowed to stay on these ranches.

Although we heard so little talk of it, we did not go entirely without art ourselves. Thus, we found in Phœnix some work by an excellent etcher, an American who is well represented in the British Museum Print

Department, who had spent many years drawing these deserts and mountains. We bought his prints there for less than we should have had to pay for them in London, in spite of the fact that nearly everything is far more expensive in the West. There was no demand for them. None of our fellow guests, capable, intelligent, elaborately educated persons, apparently cared a fig for the arts of drawing, painting, sculpture. They were much further removed from them than the ordinary Hopi Indian. They had been civilized out of the arts and not yet civilized into them again. I cannot help feeling that ordinary American men, who lead rather monotonous lives and sooner or later tend to be dissatisfied with them, miss a great deal of fun—to put it no higher than that—by accepting the tradition that there is something fancy, feminine, cissy, about the arts. Popular fiction gives the game away here. In all the really popular American novels I have read, if a man begins to talk about art— and nearly always he waves long white hands and is fond of bad French—you may be sure he is an unsympathetic character, who will shortly try to lure the women away from their duty and their he-men. A few really good artists, virile fellows, ought to be taken round all the small American towns in a sort of circus. It ought to be widely demonstrated that a first-rate creative artist can put in a day's work that would make the average business man seem like an inmate of a convalescent home. The ordinary American ought to be

made to realize that all kinds of mysterious aches, longings, bits of happiness, the odd effect of some trees or
a patch of color in the sky, are not part of some personal
weakness or eccentricity that it would be folly to mention, but are part of our common human heritage, and
that artists are the eager, lively, cunning men who go
to work with this material. They ought to understand
too that although women perhaps never lose touch with
these things as completely as some men do, there is
nothing particularly feminine about the arts, which indeed very much belong to the masculine half of the part-
nership. They ought to be shown that an artist's personal
vision of the world is at least as amusing and exciting
as another man's style of playing baseball or poker.
It is not a matter of uplift, culture, the higher things:
the argument can be kept at a brutally low level. Life
plus art is a durned sight more fun than life without
art. And the ordinary American male, I believe, can
do with some more fun. He starts off with enormous
zest, but as he gets older he finds himself going the
same old monotonous round of work and pleasure. He
ought to be told that the art of painting will put ten
thousand more windows into his house, and that through
them he will catch glimpses of a new earth and perhaps
a new heaven. Some people are really dead long before
they are dropped into their graves. But the American
at his worst is never that; somewhere inside the hard
crust that routine and an unimaginative way of life have

grown on him, he is still alive, wondering, a bit wistful; he is rather bleakly puzzled to know why he has conquered so much to feel so poor a sense of triumph; and among other things he needs art, the glorious company of the masters, not doled out to him in sips by feeble superior persons, born to be interior decorators, but pushed under his nose by men who are obviously more alive than he is. The day that five American citizens out of ten suddenly realize that a picture or a print can be as exciting as a new automobile or set of golf clubs, something will happen in all the galleries and studios in the world, thousands of good craftsmen will think the Golden Age has dawned again, and perhaps another Renaissance will arrive, as shattering as an earthquake and as good as a Christmas present.

Remote from the symphony orchestras, and away from our own wireless and gramophones, we missed music most. I do not think these Westerners realize yet how cunningly the best music can be reproduced now. Indeed, I do not think there is the same cult of the gramophone, among lovers of serious music and not merely among youngsters who want a noise and a dance, in America as there is now in England, where recently improved instruments, both of the older acoustic kind and the new kind that are combined with wireless, and a large library of electrically recorded disks, have encouraged owners of gramophones to feel they are almost running their own concert-halls. I know that I

used to be a most passionate concert-goer and haunter
of opera houses—I once attended eleven consecutive
opera performances—but now I make my own programs
at home, and though the performances are not quite so
vivid and exciting, I can choose them myself, and they
are free from that prima-donna silliness, that gasping
over-enthusiasm, which still runs riot in big concert-
halls. What we need now is a tiny portable instrument,
to which one listens through earphones, so that it does
not disturb anybody else, and whole symphonies and
concertos and operas recorded on miniature reels of film,
so that they could easily be carried about with us. Then
we could lie in bed at sea or in the desert, and still have
our music. For my part, I no longer want the huge
doses of music, the orgies of sound, that I seemed to
need once. When I was in my teens, and would sit in
the shilling gallery, peering down at old Richter taking
the Hallé Orchestra through Beethoven, Brahms and
Wagner, or occasionally staring entranced at the pale
dynamic Nikisch handling the London Symphony Orchestra, I would come reeling down that long stone
flight of stairs, drunk with music, my head starrier than
the night with tunes. When I fumbled, as I did for
hours, with piano arrangements of the great works, I
could hear again the strings fiercely cutting out their
arabesques, the wood wind mischievously gurgling and
piping, the brass pronouncing doom, the definitive clash
of the cymbals (and oh!—to be that lucky tympanist

[159]

who, in the Meistersingers Overture, at the climax, when all the noble themes have entwined themselves and gone spiraling to the heavens, calmly rises, picks up his two great disks of bronze, and then, to set the final seal, to let you know there is no more to be said or felt about this glorious matter, brings them together in a solitary but completely satisfying *cla-ash!*), and I was intoxicated all over again. The sight of a symphony orchestra in those days filled me with the deepest satisfaction; I would count every man of them carefully, to see that no tricks were being played on me, and then when I was sure they were all there, I was happy, and blessed all those benefactors who had thought of adding another ingenuity of wood or metal, until this huge instrument of wizardry had been achieved; and then I would look about me at my fellow townsmen sitting there, some of them—for we know about music in Yorkshire—already glancing at their scores, and my heart would warm to them as fellow communicants; and then I would be lost in the magic landscapes of sound, would sail great seas and find lost cities in remotest forests, would stand on moonlit turret roofs with bewitching princesses, would romp hugely with drunken giants, would fling myself down in tears by the grave of the whole beautiful world; and then down the steps I would reel again, and the cold night air would sober me a little, but only so that I felt a noble youth, ready to dedicate his life to some equally noble but rather mysterious cause, like the hero of an old and foolish romance. That is how it seems to me now, twenty-odd years and a world away, now that I am no longer the hero but only what is called the central character—for that we cannot escape—of a rather sardonic modern novel about a middle-aged author. I know so much more than he did. But even already I am beginning to see that he knew things that somehow I have since forgotten.

Because I wanted so much music then, I want so much less now. I have always had a greedy, sensual, gorging habit with beautiful sound. My mind will repeat a lovely theme over and over again, so that I have spent whole days in the recurring rhythm of one little tune, and then suddenly I will weary of the thing and try to dismiss it forever. There are many noble pieces of music with which I have long reached a kind of saturation point. Some Beethoven slow movements, which I listened to once in ecstasy, now seem like an old man's stories, shockingly long-winded, that one has heard far too often. There are whole symphonies and concertos, to say nothing of trios and quartets, that have ceased to mean anything to me, not because I have more music in me than their composers had, but because, as an idle listener, who brings little exact knowledge to his listening, I sucked all the marrow out of their bones long ago and now there seems no sustenance in them for me. But what feasts I have had! And how, even yet, the spell returns! An unfamiliar record is placed on the turntable, or the wireless is casually switched on, and then perhaps something happens that makes all the sister arts seem the dimmest transcriptions of the inner life. What a lift you get then! And then I remembered the very last time I had seen Arnold Bennett, whose death was reported to me, months and months afterwards, by a ship's wireless officer the morning we landed at Tahiti. Toscanini had just given us a superb performance of the *Eroica*, all air and fiery wonders, and we were straggling out of the Queen's Hall when I jostled Bennett, who rarely missed a first-class concert. "Ye-es, Priestley," he croaked triumphantly, in that queer rusty, choked voice of his, "it l-l-lifts you up, l-lifts-you-up." And I never saw him again, but I am glad to think we parted forever in this life to the dying echo of great music.

To this day, although I have given more time and patient attention to other things, music still seems the most potent and magical of the arts—and the strangest, the hardest to account for on any cheap, cocksure, salts-and-electricity theory of life. It is at once mathematical and mystical. It has only the slenderest roots in the ground. It is magnificently and almost insolently non-utilitarian. If the world does not welcome it, so much the worse for the world. The other arts, even at their highest reach, remain life-size, recognizably human in their scale, but to me all music worth the name is curiously larger than life, celebrating the triumphs and disasters of demigods, the fall of the Titans, the splendors of Olympus. Its joy and its anguish are keener than ours. It reports events of a magnitude beyond our understanding. We sit listening to it, moved but bewildered, as if we were the mere dogs in some great house of weddings and funeral services. Instead of diminishing life, as so much knowledge seems to do now, music magnifies it until we feel like the travelers in the Harz Mountains who see their vast shadows moving in the mist. A Beethoven seems the most terrifying, though also the noblest, of all wizards, for he projects his dreams on to the sky, which is crowded with his armies hurrying to their doom, with his dancing giants, his choirs of angels.

This noble magnitude of life that music conjures for us out of its cunning arrangement of vibrations may have no reference beyond itself and the entranced ear. It may have no more meaning than the noise of gnats, just as we ourselves may possibly be nothing much better than longer-lived and heavier gnats. The triumphant finale of the Ninth Symphony may go pealing out into a cold and empty universe. When we imagine, under the spell of this strange art, that we are beginning to catch glimpses of a life with a range and passion and beauty far beyond our own, yet linked to ours, are hearing voices from behind the veil, we may be enjoying one of the most idiotic of our illusions. Music and the final facts may have no common ground. But if this should be so—and I will accept no proofs from those who make nothing of music—if this world is only a cozy hive of illusion in a universe waiting to strip and freeze it, if Bach and Mozart, Beethoven and Brahms, in the bleak stare of reality, were only so many buzzing gnats, if the final hosannas are like the shouts of a man standing in an Antarctic night asking for wine and lights, even then the grandeur of this art must remain undimmed. We cannot say it has lied to us. If the universe is a vast mechanical nothing, incapable of sending an answering hail to the final chords of the Ninth Symphony, then our life and not that senseless engine is the real universe, which has not existed in vain for it has produced things of supreme value—there being no other values elsewhere to challenge comparison—and among those things, still triumphant, still faintly vibrating in the freezing air long after we are all dead, with the last vibration trembling on the edge of universal death, is the Ninth Symphony. Therefore, until we receive a plain message from God to go and do something better, we must make music. I think I was too long without it all this winter. Many a time I badly needed a glimpse of that larger life, a whisper from behind the veil. Remote from those tragic mad sounds, I was neither as happy nor as sane as I might have been.

Chapter Ten

AMONG the litter of papers waiting to be burned were some long sheets of typescript, and as I glanced through them before popping them into the stove, I began thinking about Hollywood, for these sheets had come from there. I had been to Hollywood before this winter; my first visit was in the spring of 1931, after I had returned from the South Seas; but I had never done any work there, having refused many excellent offers. My reason for refusing was not any lack of interest in films, for I think I am more interested in films than many writers who have worked in Hollywood for years, and I had done a certain amount of not very ambitious film work in England. But when the various offers had been made, either I did not want at the time to leave England for California for several months or I felt that I would never be able to endure the Hollywood method of working. A popular author has to swallow a good deal of his pride when he becomes part of a great film organization, because very soon he is made to realize that he is not the important fellow he imagined he was in the outside world. He is of less consequence than the producers and assistant producers, the directors, the stars, the more important featured players, the head camera men; and though he may be better paid, his standing in most studios is about that of an assistant director or camera man, a make-up man, or some of the boys in the publicity department. Often there is no reason why he should have any standing at all.

We all know those comic stories about Hollywood and its authors, who are invited out there, given gigantic sums of money, and then left to droop and wonder in silence for months. Some of them are true. But in fairness it should be remembered that Hollywood might have a different story to tell, that many popular and highly-paid authors are useless in film work because the stories they invent do not lend themselves to film treatment, they cannot write dialogue that can be heard with conviction and pleasure, and remain ignorant of film technique. Even Hollywood producers do not enjoy spending large sums of money on nothing. The mistake that they—or the heads of their scenario departments—tend always to make is to be too impulsive and not sufficiently discriminating in their offers to authors. They ought to have realized by this time that the ability to write a popular novel or even a successful play does not automatically include within itself the ability to write well for films, an entirely different medium. They should examine the work of these authors with more care. Thus, a writer who has made his reputation on a very charming narrative style or a trick of

whimsical comment and reflection will probably be useless in films because he has nothing of his own that they
can use. On the other hand, a novelist who handles broad
masses of life pictorially and has a sharp eye for a scene
is probably more than halfway towards being a first-
class scenario writer. A little elementary discrimination
of this kind would have saved Hollywood millions of
dollars and saved some of its contracted authors months
of vexation.

Having a whole winter to spend in the neighborhood,
I had decided that this time I would creep quietly into
Hollywood, see a friend or two there, and discover if
they had anything to offer me that would not interfere
too much with my plans. When I had nine people to
keep at Arizona rates, which are not modest, and some
expenses still running on in England, some extra money
would be welcome; and while earning it, perhaps I could
catch a glimpse or two of Hollywood methods of production and learn more about this new medium. I
hoped later on to create films in England, really create
them and not merely rough out scenes or add bits of
dialogue, and this brief experience might be valuable. I
might despise individual films themselves and most of
the people who were so proud of having made them, but
I was not stupid enough to despise the actual medium.
The film seemed to me a most important and fascinating
method of communication. And for two good reasons.
First, the astonishing width of its appeal. I knew that

[167]

in Great Britain alone about twenty million visits to the pictures take place every week. The figures for the rest of the world were staggering. Some men have the right to say that this means nothing to them, but not a man with my opinions. If there was ever a chance of doing a decent job for those twenty millions, I wanted to be in a position to take it. They appeared to like a good deal of cheapness and silliness that did not appeal to me —though they took an authentic genius like Chaplin to their hearts very soon—but that did not mean they would never care for anything better. In fact, there were definite signs that they would. I believed that people's taste improved, almost in spite of themselves. Especially when most of these millions *wanted* to see films, and not merely didn't mind if they did see them. Which brought me to the second reason why I did not despise films. I was fascinated and deeply impressed by their astonishingly rapid development. Novels and plays, pictures and music of twenty years ago, do not seem very different from the creations of this year, but films of twenty years ago seem genuine primitives, almost prehistorical. We take this progress for granted, but it is a rare occurrence in our history, such a dazzling advance. It happened when the popular Elizabethan drama went soaring from *Roister-Doister* to *Twelfth Night*.

And I could not agree that the creation of films was not an art at all, only an industry. It is actually a curiously mixed activity, coming into a new category, heeding all the resources and organization of a large industry, but by no means devoid of genuine artistic impulses. You have only to talk to representative producers, directors, players, and scenario-writers to discover that they too, like novelists and dramatists, painters and sculptors, can be set alight by an idea. I do not believe that the huge public cared much about what is sometimes called Film Art, the set of visual values and its accompanying technique that fascinate young men who belong to Film Societies. That public looked to films for general entertainment, on a scale hitherto unknown, and accepted the moving pictures as a substitute for theaters, books, gossip, and dreams. The stars became symbolic figures to the multitude. And some hunger that appeared to know no barrier of race was partly satisfied by this new form of entertainment. Millions of money were spent on publicity, but the big public, and especially the younger members of it, ran to meet the publicity men more than halfway. They actively, almost passionately, wanted films, more and more and more of them, and you could no more stop them with a few cultured sneers than you could stop Niagara by telling it that it was in bad taste. Here, it seemed to me, was a huge spontaneous world movement, and I saw more in it to wonder at than to despise.

I thought about the fantastic atmosphere of this film world of Hollywood, and tried to explain it to myself. It had been brought into existence by unusual but not mysterious conditions. First, there were the magnates, that serio-comic group. Most of them had been humble, ill-educated aliens, who perhaps enjoyed moving pictures all the more because they were not fully articulate in any known language, and who had suddenly found themselves high in the air on magic beanstalks, or whirled from three back rooms in Brooklyn to a pseudo-Spanish castle in Southern California. I had met a few members of this Old Guard of Hollywood, and had found them unique in their mixture of shrewdness and ignorance, bombast and humility, showmen who had had to juggle with millions, emperors of make-believe, tailors turned caliphs. Their presence alone, at the head of affairs, would explain the fantastic quality of this world. But they were not the whole of it. Once the films became popular and made fortunes, the men and women of the Theater swarmed in, led by all the swaggering mountebanks of the profession. Now in the Theater, which feeds on emotions and cares little for common sense, temperament runs riot; it is a place of gigantic quarrels, sulks, furies, reconciliations, kisses, tears, of ruling passions and swollen egos and soaring whims, of alternate bouts of idleness and crazy industry. There are, however, two severe checks on this Bedlam, and if it were not for them nothing would hardly ever be accomplished. The money soon begins to run out, which is the first check; and the second is, that temperament or no temperament, the box office is opening and soon an audience will be assembling in front of the curtain. But all these people of the Theater who entered the film world soon discovered that here these checks did not operate so swiftly, for now there was money to burn, and the audience was at a distance and could wait. In short, the film atmosphere is the old theatrical atmosphere but with the sky the limit. And as we know, in the earlier days, the sky was very important, hence the choice of southern California, which had the best weather in America for cowboys and bathing belles on location. Which brings us to the reason why the fantastic Old Guard and the fantastics from the Theater could now raise one another to new heights of the fantastic. They were now all together, miles and miles from anywhere, in Hollywood.

I would undertake, I told myself as I jammed a whole "rough treatment" into the stove's mouth, to explain the paradox of Hollywood in terms of its geographical position. And the paradox of Hollywood is this, that while it regards itself, with justice, as the capital of the whole film world, the leader, the big boss, and has always produced the highest average level of pictures, yet, to anybody of taste and intelligence, it has never produced the very best films, the really outstanding creations, which have come in turn from Sweden, Germany and Austria, Russia, and France, and may arrive at any moment now from England. It is certainly a fact of my experience that, the best Chaplin

[171]

pictures excepted, it has always been the European films that I have wanted to see more than once. The rare works of art in films have been European. On the other hand, Hollywood has supplied me with at least nine-tenths of the good entertainment I have had in picture theaters. Now both its strength and its weakness come from its geographical position. Hollywood is a long, long way from anywhere. That is why it has made so many good films, and why it has never made the best ones.

True, Hollywood is a suburb of a large city, Los Angeles, but Los Angeles too, is merely a place that is a long way from anywhere. Only a retired Iowan farmer would think of Los Angeles as a metropolis. It is a kind of boom town that has gone mushrooming itself for scores of miles. When you look down on its lights from the summit of Mount Wilson, you could imagine it was the capital of the world, for no city has ever before shown such lights, which blaze over a whole county. But when you travel along its immense boulevards, you feel you are looking at an immensely swollen small town. There seem to be miles and miles of unimpressive little bungalows and vacant building lots. Only at night does it lose its air of being determinedly third-rate. It has always seemed to me symbolical of an America I do not like, just as its rival, San Francisco, a real city with a sparkle and a charm of its own, has always seemed to me symbolical of an America I love, the large, hearty, devil-may-care, romantic America. Los Angeles has always appeared to me to be a city of boosters and boomers, Middle-Western farmers who have left their native shrewdness behind, bogus mystics and fortune-tellers, roaring publicity men, born comic-convention-attenders, all representative of an America I neither understand nor enjoy. I do not need to be told that there are plenty of nice, ordinary, sensible citizens there, because I have met numbers of them; but I cannot help feeling that it is not they but the others who have created the atmosphere of Los Angeles, that the sprawling city does somehow suggest this new age of ours at its silliest.

This, then, is the city of which Hollywood is a suburb, almost the tail that wags the dog. Indeed, the truest as well as the wittiest description of Los Angeles is "Six suburbs in search of a city." And, I repeat, they are all six a long way from anywhere, down there in that corner of southern California. There is something strange about that part of the world. It is a region in a moving picture. The hazy sea, the mountains that look like shabby brown skin-rugs, the crinkled desert, are not quite real. They do not take hold of the mind. They look more solid and enduring in photographs than they do in actuality. When I first entered this region, my mind may have been unconsciously dominated by the thought of Hollywood, but it did seem as if nothing down there was quite authentic. The orchards and gardens had been cunningly devised by an art director from Metro-Goldwyn-Mayer. The mountains beyond were by United Artists. The villages had come from Universal City. The boulevards were running through Paramount sets. Even the sunlight, which was pleasant but not quite the real thing, had probably been turned on by Warner Brothers. The picturesque Spanish bits had an operatic look about them, and I felt that somewhere around the corner was an operatic chorus of peasants, complete with cardboard flagons. The fruit so lusciously decorating the roadside was film fruit, meant to be photographed, not tasted. About all the little towns near Los Angeles there was a fancy fair and bazaar air, and it was impossible to believe they did solid business and that human beings were born or died in them. Even the ordinary people, coming from a queer mixture of races, did not seem like other Americans, but appeared to have developed an odd theatrical quality, as if they were all playing character parts. That is what I felt at first, and I do not feel very differently about it now. Except that now I feel there is also something disturbing about this corner of America, a sinister suggestion of transcience. There is a quality, hostile to men in the very earth and air here. As if we were not meant to make our homes in this oddly enervating sunshine. I see the fine highways, the innumerable well-built townships, the nightly blaze of electricity along the coast, but I cannot believe that mankind has made a permanent settlement. It is all a *de luxe* camping. Or the most expensive film set possible to be devised. The people were not here yesterday and will not be here tomorrow. At any moment, I feel, the earth may give a shudder or two, and the towns will collapse like card castles, the coast will be rolled up like a carpet, and southern California will be a silent desert again. It is all as impermanent and brittle as a reel of film. Nor am I alone with these fancies or premonitions. I doubt if any sensitive person who has ever stayed in this neighborhood has ever quite escaped them. They help to explain many of the follies of the region. Nobody feels quite at home and at ease there.

Here, then, is Hollywood, in the middle of this odd unreality of landscape and atmosphere, and remote from anything else. Now in Europe when you have agreed to work in films, you merely take a certain route every morning from your own front door. But in America, you cross the continent and go to Hollywood. On the way you will have to say good-by to most of the great realities of our communal life. Very soon the strife of the nations and the fluctuations of universal trade will dwindle into dim little tropics, only fit for a few hundred feet of news reel. The real roaring world will disappear behind the mountains and deserts. It will not be long before you will feel further from most of its life than if you were lounging on some South Sea Island. The head of Metro-Goldwyn-Mayer will soon seem a much more important figure than the President of the

United States himself. The great questions will suddenly change their form if not their urgency. Will Chaplin finish his new picture? Has Garbo retired to Sweden? What is the new schedule for color at Paramount? Are the musicals keeping up their grosses? Why did the director walk off the lot? Is So-and-so still feeling "that way" about Such-and-such? These are the questions now. Three thousand miles away, with so much else happening, they did not seem very important, only so much material for a film journalist's column. But now, with everything else remote, they loom gigantically. You are in a new world, where the sun is switched on and off in the studios, and the stars are so many handsome young men and women. It exists, this world, to make films. And that other, outside world exists in order to buy those films, and to provide material for still more films. Is there a threat of war, then what about another war picture? Are there Communists in China, Fascists in Spain, then what about sending a few camera men out for some good "back projection"? That, in brief, is the Hollywood point of view.

The people there cannot be justly accused of being absurdly self-centered. It is a tremendously difficult and engrossing task, this of providing entertainment for the world. And we who are not there encourage these people to believe that we are all living simply for the sake of their little shadow shows. We shower millions of dollars on them. We snatch eagerly at every bit of gossip they send out. If Cutie the Blonde cannot live any longer with Tough Guy, we ring her up from London, keeping the front page open, to learn exactly why. I suppose I must have visited dozens of American towns, but I have been asked more questions about Hollywood—and by intelligent people too—than about all the rest put together. Second-rate actresses, whose good looks have been carefully built by the make-up department and their personalities artfully created by publicity men, descend upon us as Hollywood stars and are received as if they were visiting queens. Hundreds of periodicals, circulating all over the world, do nothing but reprint odds and ends of gossipy rubbish from this one small area, as if the very contents of its dust bins—or rather, ash cans—ought to be housed in our museums. Only a saint or a Socrates could be proof against such flattery. When the victims are men on magic beanstalks, showmen, players, and the like, all remote from anything but this creation of film entertainment, they cannot be blamed if they imagine that Hollywood is the center of the world, and that when a film is made out of a play by Shakespeare, the old scribbler has at last arrived somewhere. This is the explanation of that fantastic vanity, notorious in many a funny story, which makes the Hollywood producer look a stupid fool. He is probably nothing of the kind, may often be an extremely clever man. But the situation in which he finds himself is too much for him. It is not his fault. It is the fault of the people who first chose such a remote place to make films in. And it is also our fault too, for making such a ridiculous fuss about the place.

In London and Paris and Berlin, film-making has to compete with a thousand other interests and occupations; but not in Hollywood. Once there, after crossing mountains and deserts, you must get into films, stay in films, or perish. You are, as it were, wrecked on an island that does nothing but make films. You have arrived at a place where a writer is a man who does scenarios for *motion pictures*, an artist is a man who designs sets for them, a composer is a man who writes music for them, and an actor a man who performs in them. I have often traveled up and down these hazily sunlit boulevards, immense but flavorless and phantasmal, and felt that all I could see about me was unreal, merely part of a dream life, and that the reality there was to be found in the millions of sharply-lit little photographs that were always being projected and examined by the producers and directors and cutters. I felt the same about most of the stars themselves. They were people born to achieve reality in a photograph. With ordinary persons, a photograph is a mere blurred hint of their true personality. But a film star dwindles and fades in the flesh. That is why the fuss that is made about film stars when they emerge as persons, descending upon the outer world, is so absurd and so well-spiced with irony. It is the photograph that should be waited for and cheered, not the actual person. This is particularly true of the young women, who may in reality be pleasant, handsome, intelligent actresses, but who can never in person be anything but ghosts of their screen appearances, though these in turn are only shadows. The man who can dine and dance with them at the Trocadero or the Café Lamaze in Beverly Hills will know less of their essential quality than the youth who has paid his shilling at the picture theater, to dream over them, in Liverpool or Plymouth, six thousand miles away. With them, the substance must always be less than the shadow. The film producers would like us to believe—and easily succeed in persuading most of us—that they are using the screen to convey to us a little of the essential glamour of these delicious beings, but the truth is, and nobody knows it better than the producers, that it is only on the screen that these stars really achieve glamour. Hollywood has probably more attractive-looking young people of both sexes, in proportion to population, than any other place in the world, but these are merely the raw material of its art. Sunset and Wilshire Boulevards are not alight with their romantic qualities, their witchery and glamour. The romance, the witchery, the glamour do not remain in Hollywood; they are manufactured there every day by clever men, to be packed up in cans and promptly exported.

Now Hollywood would not be able to export so much cheap glamour if it were not so far away. It steadily borrows enchantment from the distance. Over there on the Pacific Coast, it can hide a Garbo among its shabby-brown-fur hills, and make her as romantically inaccessible as the Grand Lama. The English film companies do not seem to realize that this remoteness is important. They bring expensive glamorous Hollywood stars to London, and then immediately let them loose in the town, allow them to spend night after night going to theaters and restaurants and private parties, where the crowds see them and the pressmen take their usual unflattering snapshots. This is bad business. If Garbo put in six months running around the West End of London every night, at the end of the period she would seem to the English public about as mysteriously remote as the local Town Clerk. With the English public, films made in London will never be able to compete in the romantic glamour department with those made in far-away Hollywood. English film producers should not waste money and time trying to compete on these lines, but should try for a special appeal and excellence of their own. Nobody will beat the Hollywood boys on their own ground. The advantages that have naturally followed from its geographical position will always belong to it. And we have now seen what they are. Glamour by way of remoteness is one of them. So is the concentration upon film-making because there is so little else to do and think about there. And the belief that humanity has been specially created to make and

take films. The high technical skill of Hollywood may
be due in part to American wealth and organization
and fondness for teamwork, but it is also partly the
result of this isolation. What a happy choice of locality?
It looks as if, in this game, Hollywood holds all the
kings and aces.

There are, however, some very good cards it will
probably never hold. There are some drawbacks to this
geographical position. It is too far from the main stream
of life. The line of communication between Hollywood
and the real world of politics, economics, industry, art,
philosophy, religion, is much too long and attenuated.
After all, even films have to take some nourishment
from reality, and Hollywood is too far away to be properly nourished. In that strangely enervating sunshine,
which seems to produce flowers without scent and fruit
without flavor, a sterile influence is perpetually at work.
Hollywood has not the rich soil necessary for a fine
healthy crop of art. It summons men of talent from
the ends of the earth, flatters and feasts them and gives
them millions of dollars to play with, but somehow the
originality and gusto and fertility of most of these men
soon desert them in the Hollywood studios. The money,
the organization, all the technical resources, the tremendous concentration of interest, have all been there,
but you need more than these to create a work of art,
as distinct from a slick mechanical piece of entertainment.
Producers of films should be inspired by the great spec-

tacle of this life, moved by it to compassion, laughter and wonder, and a producer in London, Paris, or Moscow, has this great spectacle roaring around him day and night, can dive at any hour into a vast invigorating sea of life, can bring up treasures from the deep. But in Hollywood, which is a mountain of celluloid, there is only a thin over-worked seam of real life. So Hollywood shows us the egoism of the artist but not his broad and rapturous humanity. It is too rich; it has been flattered by too many fools; and it is too remote and self-centered. And that, I concluded, is why it has done so well, and why it has never done any better.

Intelligent people, I told myself, have always tended to underrate Hollywood, just as for a long time they underrated films in general. We all know the funny stories about the Hollywood film magnates, but we are apt to forget that most of these stories are either invented or reported by other men who also belong to Hollywood. And it has always produced the best satires on itself. Rich men in the film industry are often ignorant and stupid and have far too much power, but then rich men in many other industries are often ignorant and stupid and have far too much power. That familiar criticism is really one of the capitalist system, not specially of Hollywood. We can see that in films the man who controls the purse does not necessarily make a good leader. But why only in films? Perhaps I had heard too many of these funny stories, but certainly

I had always been surprised by the quick intelligence of most of the people I had met in Hollywood. They were not quite the tremendous fellows they obviously thought they were, but they were not the ignorant buffoons and mountebanks they are so often reported to be. I had been often impressed by their knowledge of and deep interest in the new art of the film. Often they knew and loved what was good, even if they did not try to create it themselves. Their trouble was that they had been caught up in a machine that belonged to industry, not to art. In order to pay their way, they had to please the millions in all the American small towns, and that meant they had to turn out something that would amuse a not very bright boy or girl of about fifteen. Impose the same limitation on books and plays, and the result would be more disastrous still. With films costing so much to produce, the appreciation of a limited public, fully adult persons, merely meant ruin. Unfortunately, the addition of sound, bringing in a new army of technical men and a demand for still more elaborate studios, had horribly enlarged those costs. And there had been in Hollywood—and in all the film communities that imitate Hollywood—a ridiculous tradition of reckless expenditure, partly based on the vulgar notion that a film that cost a million dollars must be better than one that cost half as much.

But the public must take some of the blame for this idiocy, as it must for many others, such as the monstrous

star system. By this time the public should be proof
against the vulgarest sort of publicity. It has had years
now in which to consider its relation to the film, and
yet it still flocks into the super-of-super cinema to see
the super-of-super film, and refuses to risk its pennies
in a place that looks less like a wedding cake, to see a
more intelligent piece of entertainment. If the big
publics wanted something better, Hollywood could and
would give it to them. Not that the people do not learn
anything. They cannot visit picture theaters year after
year without learning something, and though there
may be no marked improvement in those purely cine-
matic values that young men write books about, there
is a steady demand for better writing, direction, acting,
in films. But the progress is slow, and must be while
films are so expensive to make that they must have
the approval of all the small town adolescents. I knew
that some of the best pictures Hollywood had done,
such as *The Thin Man*, had cost only a fraction of the
fabulous sums associated in the public mind with the
production of films. But there had been no general effort
to bring down costs all round, to make films for various
limited publics just as there are plays and books for
various limited publics. And here, I felt, these men I
met in Hollywood, though so much more intelligent,
knowledgeable and sensitive than they are commonly
supposed to be, had failed us, and that behind the
burnished screen of tough cynicism, which made them

[184]

such amusing talkers, they were constantly disturbed by this sense of failure. They could make me feel still young and foolish, but I fancied that there remained in me a certain creative zest, which keeps one young and possibly foolish, that had been withered away in them.

There was indeed, I remembered, something curiously withering about Hollywood. I had never stayed long enough in it myself to be unhappy there, and had more than one very pleasant stay. One week we spent there this winter, just before Christmas, had been delightful. H. G. Wells had suddenly popped up, and we had had an entrancing evening with him and Charles Chaplin. Our old friend, Hugh Walpole, whom we had met off and on all winter, was there, a rosy piece of England. There was a droll evening of dining and boxing in the company of two of the Marx brothers. The producer with whom I was associated at the time, Arthur Hornblow of Paramount, who is as energetic and efficient in hospitality as he is in production (and he made *Ruggles of Red Gap*), had found amusing and decorative company for us and some good tennis for me. Edmund Gwenn and Nigel Bruce and other not unhappy exiles from the London stage and the Garrick Club entertained us. Remembering these smiling hosts, I saluted them, but told myself to drop this catalogue of hospitality received, which was rapidly taking on the tone of a vote of thanks, unpleasantly spiced with the flavor of a Hollywood gossip writer's column. We had

had a delightful time. And that week the place was looking its best, because it was decorated for Christmas, with illuminated trees all along Hollywood Boulevard. In the Paramount Studio, where I did some work, there was a glorious Christmas tree, lit with scores of blue bulbs, a fine Hans Andersen piece of decoration.

So charmingly spangled, under clear night skies, and with every shop window stuffed with gifts and brilliantly illuminated all night, Hollywood did for once look the fairy-tale place that it appears to be in the imagination of thousands of youngsters all over the world. For the first time, I wondered if it would not be fun to work and live there for a fairly long spell. For once, I was really tempted. The sunshine, the spangled nights, the easy money, the publicity-fed glamour of these names and faces, the amusing cynical talk—it would all be fun. This was Hollywood as it really was, and no wonder that So-and-so and Such-and-such—good dramatists and actors, who had had their successes in London—preferred it to our distant fog and gloom and formality. The place made me feel vaguely uneasy before simply because I did not know it. There was too, I decided, a sort of baffled vanity behind my suspicion and faint dislike, because here in this film world, with its strange film values, I did not seem sufficiently important. I was now almost ready to envy the various friends who had their contracts with the studios and their bungalows and tennis courts out at Beverly Hills, and had settled down. It would be even more fun once we were out of the hotel, had our own place, did not notice the enormous distances between any one engagement and the next, had also settled down. I began to make vague plans to return for a long stay. And yet when it was time to leave, at the end of this brief visit, I found myself oddly ready to go.

A few weeks afterwards, I stayed just long enough in Hollywood to complete my business there, two or three days, and then fled up the coast, to Santa Barbara, to finish the piece of writing I had to do for Hollywood, a two-hour journey away from it. And I no longer had the least desire to return for a stay of months, would have paid good money to escape from any obligation to do so. The old uneasiness and suspicion were troubling me again, now that the Christmas trees and the colored lights had been packed away. There was still a fairy-tale element about the place, but now, as long before, it seemed to belong to the more sinister and menacing passages of a fairy-tale. Thus I noticed once more that the easy big money of Hollywood seemed in most people's hands—and I was sure that mine would be among them—to turn into fairy gold, which is glittering heavy metal one moment and dead leaves the next. I had never known a place in which people appeared to receive less for their money. After a few modest comforts had been paid for, princely salaries seemed to melt into air. Those who saved desperately were always unfortunate somehow in their investments. Others could not save but could only just scrape along on the combined incomes of three cabinet ministers. Yet the days when Hollywood prices were like those in some Klondike boom town had gone, along with the fantastic castles of the producers, the gold-plated motor cars of the stars, all the milk baths and feasts of peacocks and nightingales' tongues of the crazy silent picture period. Hollywood prices for most things seemed to be lower than those in London. A decent house and a good meal cost no more, and a car or the clothes demanded by the climate cost less. Taxes were high, but no higher than in England. There was no reason to be found in economics for this strange financial fatality. It was magical. A witch had cursed all the money in the place, so that no good ever came of it. In the whole history of the world there can never have been a community in which fewer people ever comfortably retired on their savings. Billions of dollars have vanished like face-cream. For years now, in these studios, which are themselves like mad towns, churches and palaces and taverns have gone up one morning and been pulled down the next, and the money they give you would seem to belong to the brief magical world of these sets rather than to the more solid and enduring world outside. Fairy gold today, and dead leaves tomorrow.

It could still be fun, however, even if its money behaved so strangely, and might indeed for a limited period be all the more fun. But that was not all. There returned to me the suspicion that you had to be a very casual visitor or to be very young and silly, to find life in Hollywood such fun. It could be gay and was undoubtedly becoming more and more intelligent, but I suspected that it was not really much fun. There was not enough security, too much competition, too many intrigues. It was, I felt, too ruthless a community. The studios found it easier to illuminate themselves with Christmas trees than with the Christmas spirit. If the history of Hollywood could be written, there would be plenty of roaring slapstick comedy in the narrative, but the final effect, I believed, would be oddly tragic. Too many of these people found themselves sliding along tightwires above a black pit of poverty, idleness and oblivion. The atmosphere was too often like that of the court of some half-crazed despot; a dark look, a whisper or two, and then the guards led you out. There had always been this tragic uncertainty in the world of the Theater, where so many players smiled and bowed in the lights for a little while and then spent years out of them nursing a heartache. But the Theater at its worst, I felt, was far less arbitrary and merciless than Hollywood. Not the individuals there (though some of them were tough enough), but the film industry. It made no allowances, felt no pity. It watched the public as an executioner might watch a sultan; a twitch of that thumb, and you were doomed. And there is a certain

[189]

streak of disloyalty, capriciousness, cruelty, in the American public, which enjoys crowning a favorite but equally enjoys stripping and banishing that favorite. To this public, Hollywood was too conscientious a servant. A boy or girl could arrive here to land among the sudden splendors, the magical generosity, of an Arabian fairy tale; but if the jewels and palaces appeared like Aladdin's, they could also vanish like Aladdin's, leaving the youngsters that owned them stranded on the desert, listening to the howls of malicious invisible *genii*. They did not all have to worry; the minor technicians and the workmen in the studios seemed lively lads; certain old stagers, "featured players" of a very definite type, appeared to have settled down cozily in the place; and various experts, confident in their skill, had clearly arrived at their Mecca. But most of the others in this community were not at home and at ease. Some of them were "out," that is, Hollywood no longer wanted them, had told them plainly it no longer wanted them; but they hung on, cursing the place but unable to leave it. Others were "in," were gay, rich, envied, flattered, but somehow were not having much fun, and had to do something dangerous or showy or messy, had to be drunk and noisy at parties, or dash about in high-powered cars, or entangle themselves in the most complicated matrimonial affairs, just to prove that they really were having a wonderful time. And though I like films, I found I had no great desire to join this life of

[190]

theirs. My first impression had been right. Hollywood was not for me.

This, I concluded, was easily the strangest corner of the world I had ever known. It has the sea and the mountains and never-failing sunshine, and yet so little charm. Men I had known in England had come out here to work, had turned up in these studios, as bronzed and fit and smiling as royal personages in the Press, to tell me they never felt so well before, and then had died quite suddenly. Everybody here is bronzed and fit, and nobody seems quite healthy. The climate suggests that it is the best in the world to work in, yet somehow one can do twice as much work almost anywhere else. There is no more cosmopolitan place than this, and yet it still seems an American small town suffering from elephantiasis. These endless boulevards are swarming now with artists of every kind, yet there is hardly a glimmer of real art. The most beautiful women in the continent live here, yet one can hardly bother looking at them. People spend fortunes on entertaining, yet there is still not one really first-class hotel or restaurant in the place. It is the only town I have ever been in where visitors are solemnly conducted on sight-seeing tours of "homes," and yet there is probably no town in which there are fewer real homes. It is a community of "wonderful lovers" who have neither the time nor the inclination to make love, a Venusberg that will not admit Venus. Its trade, which is in dreams at so many dollars a thousand feet, is managed by business men pretending to be artists and by artists pretending to be business men. In this queer atmosphere, nobody stays as he was; the artist begins to lose his art, and the business man becomes temperamental and unbalanced. Nearly every service is badly performed—the chauffeurs are careless, the cooks are casual, the chambermaids cannot dust, the waiters cannot wait—because so many of these people are aspirants who are not allowed to act or write scenarios and will not bother to learn how to do anything else properly. There is no place where you get more money, and no place where you get less value for it. The whole world is entertained by it, but it can only laugh bitterly at itself. And—last paradox of all— such roots as this film colony has are in a community even more fantastic than itself; for once the citizens are crazier than the actors; and only the wildest make-believe of Hollywood can express the astonishing reality of Los Angeles.

Yes, some of the comic films do it. Not Chaplin's. The films of that laughable sad little man, that wistful tatterdemalion with the ridiculous feet and the haunted eyes, a symbolic figure half French, half English, and not at all American, have a finer and truer genius of clowning than any others. They brought into this new medium the humor that shines forever in Shakespeare and Dickens, but they did not bring it directly but by way of an institution that Shakespeare and Dickens would have loved, the English music-hall, where I as a boy had seen Chaplin, a youth, play in the old Karno sketches. I remembered how Chaplin and I had talked of this pre-war music-hall, and how he had lightly sketched, in grimace, gesture, voice, some of the drolls we both recollected. (Chaplin is the best mimic I have ever known.) We exchanged snatches of the old songs. There was one fine Cockney lyric, called "Three pots a shilling," all about the joys of a day in the country with your girl and some beer, and as I remembered it, in the silence of that Arizona midnight, months afterwards, I could hear again Chaplin's pleasant Cockney lilt, and I remembered then how delighted I had been —and secretly a little moved, too—by that foolish popular song of yesterday, by its essentially English innocence and clear charm, which stole into that hard noisy Hollywood restaurant like a waft of the scent of hay, and suddenly made me sick to be home again. The little men that Chaplin creates for us, to laugh and cry over, are figures from his own youth, and they belong to London and Liverpool, not to New York and Los Angeles. One scene he played—in a picture of his best period, when he could do what he wanted but was not yet too self-conscious, called *Pay Day*—has remained in my memory as the perfect expression in pantomime of the dumb pathos of those millions in the vast drab dormitories of industrial England. Charlie has been celebrating, not very successfully, his pay night; and now it is late, and raining in the dark empty streets, and the evening is over. He tries to catch the last tram, but being the first inside is pushed clean out of the other end, back into the street again. The tram goes. He turns away, faintly jaunty, and begins to walk home, the solitary little figure disappearing into the dark rainy gulf between the warehouses. It ought to have been a great riotous night, but somehow it wasn't; and now he has to trail home, where a large angry wife is waiting for him; and tomorrow he will be on short rations again and back at work; and it is all very disappointing yet not quite hopeless, for some belated miracle might happen, some moon of romantic adventure peep over the high roofs and brighten the rain. All this is expressed by that dwindling little figure, and twenty Marxian treatises about the proletariat would not make you feel a tenth of the compassion for the dispossessed urban masses as this bit of pantomime does. That is the genius of Chaplin, but it seems to me to have little to do with America. He himself is one of the oldest inhabitants of Hollywood, but never in spirit has he lived there. It is simply the place where he goes to work, as another might go to work in a factory. He may live in California and dream of Moscow, but in spirit he still belongs to the East End of London, to the swarms of bright-eyed urchins who are thumbing their noses at the nearest policeman. And he remains the greatest English humorist since Dickens.

[194]

No, I thought, the task of commenting, by way of comic make-believe, on the idiocies of the life around them has been left to such newer film drolls as the Marx Brothers. They came to Hollywood from Broadway and the vaudeville circuits, but their wildly extravagant films are a roaring satire on that America which expresses itself without restraint in such a city as Los Angeles. They are southern California typified in the antics of three very different but brilliant buffoons. Chico is the bewildered, rather sullen, Latin type of peasant who has found his way to these shores, and is lost because he has left one civilization and cannot find another to replace it. Harpo, who never speaks and does just what he pleases, who has a passion for wanton destruction, who never sees a pretty girl without dropping everything and making straight for her, is the Unconscious at play, the ordinary citizen in dreams and with the lid off. Groucho—my own favorite, and, without his property mustache and cigar and baggy clothes, a sensitive and intelligent companion—is the outrageously impudent and loquacious caricature of all bogus American glad-handing politicians, real-estate boomers, Rotarians, Kiwanis, yapping know-alls, smart alecks, and the rest. In one mad sequence, he will give you half a dozen of these types and along with them his criticism of them. Together, these wild buffoons, apparently asking for nothing but the shortest cut to a laugh, contrive in their films to produce the most

[195]

searching parody of that American life which has flowered so gigantically in the neighboring city of Los
Angeles. Our grandmothers used to believe that a
thoughtful Nature always put the antidote near the
poison, so that close by the nettles there grew the dock
leaves that would ease the sting. It would seem as if that
Nature had been at work here. You could begin the
day by attending the strange festivities of the Los
Angeles Breakfast Club, go to worship under the guidance of Aimee Semple Macpherson, pass the afternoon
at whatever idiotic convention was being held, and then
at the end of a day of solemn clowning go and see the
deliberate clowning of a Marx Brothers film and thus
be purged.

In the ordinary life of this region, especially among
the poorer folk, there are unmistakable signs of something
new coming into the world. The very streets, with their
flimsy, gaudy little booths that sell hamburgers and
iced drinks, have a look of their own. Everywhere you
cannot help feeling that you have wandered into some
gigantic fancy fair or exposition ground. Nothing is
built to last, but plenty of bright paint is splashed about.
The general effect is not unlike that of a slightly shabby
toyshop. In some parts of the world, an equable climate, with months of steady sunshine, has produced a
slow dignity, but not here. I remembered driving along
one of these roads with a Hollywood friend, a very
intelligent producer, and I remarked on the odd appear-

ance to me of the road and its buildings, the slap-dash cheap picturesqueness of the whole scene and its suggestion of a free-and-easy instability. All new to me, I added, and unlike anything else I had ever seen. "Yes," he had replied, "they're new people here, not like any other kind. Quite different from the other Americans. I've found that out. Very curious. The point is," he had said in conclusion, "they don't give a damn." At the time, I remembered, I had felt I knew exactly what he meant by that. Since then I had seen more of them, though not a great deal. Did I still know exactly what he meant?

I began to think about the chauffeur we had employed this winter for some short periods in Hollywood. (The distances are so great and the topography so confusing that a chauffeur who knows the district is very useful.) Actually he had been born in the Middle West, but somehow to me he typified the southern Californian of the poorer classes. What he amounted to racially I did not know; but there was a bit of Russian, a bit of Polish, in him; though he had no accent but his now native American. Like many other southern Californians, he suggested a hearty and careless mixture of races. The result was that he seemed neither ordinary American nor distinctively alien, but some new thing between the two, again like so many of the others. He was a friendly chap, without that half-arrogant, half-shy aloofness of so many chauffeurs, and neither servile nor aggressively

[197]

your equal in the great democracy. There was perhaps a certain softness about him. He did the job he was paid for, did it well and willingly, but you knew he liked to take things easily. And you felt that he was casual about nearly everything, never worrying about what he would be doing next year, vaguely confident that something would be always turning up. A great deal of money might not take you very far in southern California, but on the other hand you can also make do on very little. You and your wife and children do not need many clothes, and mostly those of the cheap cotton variety; you can live in a shack, and hardly need fuel; and for twenty-five cents you can buy an armful of fruit and vegetables. And if you want to have a *beano*, you can buy a gallon jar of Californian wine, which is potent and not undrinkable, for a couple of dollars or so. You cannot exist without a motor-car of some sort, but you can pick up some rattletrap of an old Ford for next to nothing and gasoline is cheap enough. And there is always the sunshine, in which your children can play and you can sit and blink.

If I were condemned to poverty in America, I would go to southern California, if I had to walk there. To be wretchedly poor in New York or Philadelphia or Chicago is like being poor in London, Liverpool or Glasgow, it is hell, for you need so much, by way of shelter, fuel, food, and clothes, that only money can buy. Poverty in the sunlight is a different matter, and merely comparative. The local politics are fierce enough down there, competing in the scandal sheets with all the local murders, rapes, kidnapings, and Hollywood divorces, but you seem well out of the way of the sinister main stream of world politics. There are aircraft and cruisers at Wilmington and San Diego to protect you from the Japanese, but as the Japanese are thousands of miles away, not glowering over a frontier, you do not spend much time wondering how well you will be protected. And though the dollars keep thinning out, and the taxes increase, and if you should ever go on strike they may beat you up, you get by, and there is always the possibility that your eldest daughter, who is dead set on it, may become a film star. Easy-going, brown-faced, picturesquely dressed folks, who have wandered far from Puritanism and rugged individualism and keep-working-till-you-drop ethics, dwellers on the slopes of the celluloid volcano of Hollywood, new people with your *Twentieth-century American Pacific Type* labels still wet, where are you going, and what accomplishment, what character, will come out of you in the end?

Before the Hollywood scripts in the stove were all ashes, there came then a last memory, one of those vivid little flashes that seem to have an odd significance. Once more we were driving at night along Sunset Boulevard, almost in midair it seemed, towards Beverly Hills, to dine perhaps at the "Trocadero" or the "Victor Hugo." The night was an immense velvet jewel-case

[199]

in which a million multicolored gem-like points caught some distant light. Still higher, on our right, were the signaling mountains. Far below on our left was the twenty-mile winking glitter of Los Angeles. All so new, strange, impressive; we might have been going out to dinner in Atlantis. And there, ahead of us, I saw once more the large sign, so urgent against the velvet darkness in its red neon light: *Psychologist*. Once more, it disappeared, and I thought I had imagined it. Once more, it flashed on again, its wealth of red neon more compelling than twenty traffic signals: *Psychologist*. There it was, blazing away. If you wanted a psychologist at once, in the dead of night, here he was, waiting for you. Once more, I felt like a man in a dream; all was new; strange, and impressive; and at every moment, all was becoming newer and stranger, leaping beyond any degree of impressiveness straight into wonderland, curiouser and curiouser . . .

Chapter Eleven

STILL rummaging among the papers on my second little table in the hut, not the one on which I typed, but the messy one covered with pipes and tobacco-tins and match-boxes, and paper-fasteners, I found a bundle of small sheets, with only a few words, in a large print hand, on each sheet. I recognized them as notes I had used for a speech, two months or so before. They had that air of silliness touched with faint pathos that one's notes always have. It is like seeing oneself unexpectedly in a mirror, though here—and this way explain the touch of pathos—it is a past self that is reflected. More than once I have had to examine the belongings of people very close and dear to me, just after their death, and it has been my experience that of all the things they left behind, these odd rough notes, a man's jottings for a speech or a committee meeting, a woman's list for a morning's shopping, are the most unbearably poignant. They bring back the people, almost to life, but frame them in a terrible irony. Something of that irony is with us when we come across our own scribbles. Or so it is with me, who am always alternately being a fine fellow, armored in self-esteem, and a second jeering self that disarms and then kicks out the fine fellow. The second man feels that it was the first fellow who wrote the notes and so immediately declares that they are silly, but the first fellow at once returns to hint at pathos. Hence the sudden complication of feeling.

As a rule I do not use notes in making speeches. They tend to dry you up. You find yourself neither improvising nor reading. I had found that the best method for me was to turn the subject over in my mind a few hours before I was due on the platform, to jot down a few headings, perhaps put the notes in my pocket, and then to trust to memory. Audiences do not ask for a closely-knit piece of reasoning, but they dislike a jerky hesitating manner and the frequent stops of the note-consultant. It has always been a surprise to me that audiences at lectures, meetings or public dinners, are so humble and long-suffering, ask for so little, and are so ready to magnify any crumb of oratory into a feast. Writing is difficult, and yet these same people, without knowing much about it, will criticize it very freely. They talk among themselves, and sometimes write to editors, the most dreadful bosh about prose style, coolly contradicting men who have spent half a lifetime wrestling with the difficult art of composition. Assemble them in a banqueting-hall or lecture-theater, and they will applaud and genuinely admire a bit of speech-making that is child's play compared with writing. I do not consider myself a really good speaker, if only because I have few of the tricks and none of the artful graces of the practiced orator; but, although I do not do a great deal of it, I am an effective speaker, almost certain of a hearty round, simply because I have a resonant voice, take care never to ramble dully on, and am not afraid of my audience once I am on my feet. I have learned the trick of turning off my imagination, which is always anxious to transform the waiting audience into a kind of thousand-headed monster. Obviously, the average audience is simply a collection of not very formidable individuals, most of whom are definitely on your side because, like you, they want the occasion to be a success. You can soon see this, once you have turned off your imagination. It will help if you do not try to look at the audience as a whole, but take a good look at a few individuals in it, and then ask yourself what is frightening about them. If they still look terrifying, perhaps it would be better not to speak.

These notes, however, were intended for use on the platform and that is why I had printed them boldly with my thickest and blackest pencil. For once I felt I could not trust entirely to my memory. My address would last nearly an hour and a half; I was not talking on an old subject; and anyhow I needed a number of quotations that would have to be written down. I had been asked to deliver the Convocation Address at the University of Colorado, which had chosen the same day on which to give me an honorary degree. An old friend of mine was a professor there, which probably explains both address and degree. We had arranged to stay with this friend and his wife for several days, to meet people and to look about us. We wanted to go by road from Wickenburg, Arizona, to Boulder, where the University of Colorado is, but it meant traveling hundreds and hundreds of miles among mountains thick with snow and risking being held up by a sudden blizzard. So we motored as far as the main railway line at Ash Fork, and took a train to Denver, Colorado, from there. This train journey lasted about twenty-seven hours, and at other times and places would have seemed a very formidable venture, but now in this country of enormous distances and intrepid travelers we thought nothing of it. In England our ideas of travel are carefully adjusted to the diminutive size of the island, and it is extraordinary how they naturally expand in America, and especially in the West. The town of Phœnix was over sixty miles from our ranch near Wickenburg. At one time we had lived in a village called Church Hanborough, about eight miles from Oxford. After a few weeks in Arizona, we spoke of going to Phœnix exactly as we had once spoken of going to Oxford from Church Hanborough. The five hundred miles between Wickenburg and Hollywood could be covered nicely between breakfast and tea-time—once when I had to get to the Coast in a hurry and the daily plane and the daily train had both gone, the proprietor of our ranch pushed me into his

Packard after supper and we spent the moonlit night tearing off those five hundred miles, at the rate of seventy an hour—and this journey soon seemed to us about the same as that between London and Bath. The Westerner who comes to Britain must feel he is wandering about in a toy world. We know that the American always sees the English train as a sort of fierce little toy. The American train looks three times the size, and always has the air of having just rumbled in from some quite different latitude and climate. And it always smells stuffily of people, like a small crowded hotel. This stuffiness was not unwelcome at first on our way to Denver, because it was bitterly cold among the mountains.

I could see myself then, humped up, smoking, in the parlor car, occasionally staring out at the grim wintry plateau or the far fading peaks, but mostly reading. I could remember what I was reading during that journey. It was Santayana's *The Last Puritan*, a novel that was having a great success, sharing the top place in the best-seller lists with an even worse novel, Briffault's *Europa*. Why all the American reviewers had decided that these two indifferent performances were masterpieces, and why the American public was buying them by the truckload, these were mysteries to me. I had an old admiration for Santayana and had once written about him at some length, but his novel, though it offered at times a glimpse of that distinguished mind, seemed to lack spontaneity and vitality: reading it was like loitering among tombstones. It seems to be generally overlooked now that though the art of fiction may be very rough-and-ready and by no means the fine-drawn affair that Henry James thought it was, yet it is an art, with its own absolutely essential virtues. You do not need to have a distinguished mind or a fine style to be a good novelist. If you have some notion of what philosophic thought is, so much the better, but that is not necessary, either. But you do need to be able to create characters and scenes that come alive in the reader's imagination. No creative power, no novel. And if distinguished writers who do not happen to possess this particular kind of power begin writing novels—as so many seem to do now—then not only will they produce poor lifeless specimens of fiction, but they may be depriving us of the really good work they are capable of doing well. I did not want a frigid novel from Santayana, but some more of his enchanting philosophical reveries. There were several others—poets, historians, biographers, descriptive writers—of whom I could say the same thing. It is just as if we were always arriving at concerts nowadays to discover a famous pianist trying his hand at a violin concerto. Why, then, are these tepid efforts at fiction, with good names attached to them, so often praised by critics? I concluded, after thinking about several influential critics I knew, that it was because such critics are not themselves much interested in fiction, which cannot be read in great quantities without becoming very cloying and wearisome, and are glad to welcome the good names and either do not know or have stopped caring whether the novels attached to them have life in them or not.

I had, I told myself, no particular pedantry about fiction. It is one of the vaguest forms of the art of literature, which, unlike music and painting, is not itself a pure art. I believed it was easy to overrate the importance of certain technical devices in the Novel, just as Henry James and his disciple, Percy Lubbock, had done. The point of view, the shape, the pattern, the rhythm, these count for something, but not for a great deal, and for nothing at all if the fiction itself does not come to life. A certain creative zest is essential in the novelist. An essay, a biography, a travel book, a treatise, any of them is preferable to the lifeless novel, with its characters that are mere outlines, its tedious undramatic scenes, its dialogue that never suggests living speech. I would rather have a genuine creation by a cheap little mind in fiction than a dull and frigid performance by a fine mind. And if I were an editor I would not employ a man to review fiction unless he shared this taste. The trouble with the Novel is that it is now regarded as the vast lucky dip of the literary life. Put your hand in and see what you get! Good writers of every kind, as well as a horde of people who can just put sentences together, all have a try. If the thing looked a bit more difficult to do, even the tiniest bit, half of them would not bother trying. It is very easy, of course, to have a shot at a novel, just as it is easy to have a shot at singing a song. For the last twenty years I have believed that I have a good, though completely untrained, bass singing voice, but it has never occurred to me to give a recital at the Queen's Hall. I am a fine fellow but no real singer. And George Santayana and Robert Briffault are fine fellows, too, but no novelists..

We arrived at Denver in the middle of the afternoon, and our friends were there to meet us and then motor us to their home of Boulder, thirty miles away. There was something very odd about Denver, and it was not until we had left the main streets behind that I realized what it was. Nearly all the larger towns in the West look brand new, but Denver looked comparatively old. It is. It was quite a place, with all the amenities, back in the 'seventies. Now it is the largest city between Kansas City and the Pacific Coast, a stretch of over eighteen hundred miles. But all I could remember about it, though it was not three months since I was there, was this odd impression of comparative antiquity, based on a passing glimpse of a fifty-year-old hotel or store. Nor did I remember much more of the country around it, through which we passed on our way to Boulder. We were over a mile high, and it was winter, and though the sun was shining and the air was clear, the whole land seemed to be motionless in the steel grip of January. Our way ran along a plateau, with the high peaks of the Rockies (and Colorado has about forty times as many high peaks as Switzerland) like a great icy wall on our left. At that distance from below these mountains had not the exciting thrust and romantic promise of the Alps. They looked withdrawn and severe, frozen forever. Boulder itself was at the very foot of these high slopes, where it smoked away contentedly, a cozy little town with a brownish wooden look about it, drawing its life from the university. I remember liking its appearance at once, which is more than I had done with some other American university towns, and feeling that, address or no address, I was about to enjoy myself in this place.

So it turned out. We had been staying in either guest ranches or hotels for months, and it was good to be back in somebody's home, especially when our hosts were old friends. We were hard at it arguing and gossiping before the stream of visitors arrived, and started all over again when the last of them had gone and we had dropped into chairs, exhausted. I liked what I saw of the university itself. It is fortunate in having as president a real scholar, a wise old student of the humanities, in place of the all-too-frequent Dr. Boomer. (You will find him in Leacock's *Arcadian Adventures With The Idle Rich*, that riotous satire which a surprisingly large number of intelligent persons do not appear to know.) And I could not help feeling that the remoteness of this little town and the steely presence of those mountains gave the corporate life there more ease and coziness than are usual in universities. Some of the students came from as far away as New York. Two students, one of each sex, worked as "domestic help" in the house where we stayed. I had met such students before, in various parts of America, and had always liked the look of them. American higher education may be sometimes slapdash and fantastic, with its short-story or saxophone courses, its strange fraternities and sororities, its musical-comedy co-ed atmosphere, its heavily solemn games departments; but at least it has never departed from the fine mediæval tradition of the poor scholar. If only one out of every four of these girls and young men who work their way through college succeeds in the end in being decently educated, the system amply justifies itself and does honor to the democracy that supports it. I admire a country in which it is possible to work towards a degree by washing dishes or stoking a furnace. I wish more professional men in England had at some time or other had to wash dishes or stoke furnaces. It is a weakness of our higher education that it protects its scholars only too thoroughly, so that some of them hardly know what the outside world is like. Lots of schoolmasters and clergymen have never in their lives left one section or another of the scholastic hothouse. We keep our clever boys too long at school, and then make another mistake by passing

them straight from school to a university. I have long
had a theory that the years between seventeen and
twenty might be well spent away from schools and colleges, preferably at some roughish work. I have often
thought that some form of labor corps conscription
would not be a bad thing for youngsters in their late
teens. It would help them to learn something about
their country and their future fellow citizens. At present, it is so often the professional man, urgently needing
this knowledge, who has been carefully educated in
ignorance of it.

During one of these pleasant parties, I astonished a
lady by not passionately agreeing with her about co-
education in universities. If I had said a few words in
defense of cannibalism, she could not have been more
astonished. She took it for granted that college co-
education was now beyond reasonable objection. I argued that during these three or four years it was possible to live a good life without the company of the
other sex, that its presence probably did more harm
than good, that the atmosphere of some American co-
educational institutions I had visited had seemed to me
overcharged with sexuality, that too much time and
energy were wasted on the preliminaries of courtship
(and not always the preliminaries) and the attendant
rivalries and jealousies. Youngsters of about twenty do
not greatly miss the other sex if members of it are not
on show. They are more likely to form valuable friend-

ships with other young men or women if mating is not part of the college routine. They will have plenty of time for all the complications of the sexual life after they have taken their degrees. Why not a few celibate and uncomplicated years devoted to work and play, argument and friendship? I did not add that it had seemed to me that American youngsters, especially in the Far West, plunged into the bewildering drama of sex at far too early an age, and that it was disturbing to see senior high-school boys and girls behaving, over midnight cocktails, like rather unscrupulous amorists of forty. If boys of nineteen needed a strong coarse mixture of blatant sex and booze, when they ought to be at the idyllic age, what was to happen to them later on in middle life? Having arrived at manhood with the habits of gay dogs of fifty, what will they be like after another thirty years, when they are fifty? Will they be retired sour sensualists by that time? Or will they be wanting something very fierce and rank indeed to amuse them? Meanwhile, I could not see that co-education in college would do them any good at all.

As I talked with these various amiable professors, I remember that I began to wonder what sort of professor I would have made. I had had my chances. During my final year at Cambridge and for one or two years afterwards, I had the usual opportunities of applying for very rum remote professorships, most of them in the new Baltic states, in the Orient, or in one of the wilder provinces of Canada. As I had no job and no money, I was tempted once or twice to apply, but never got so far as demanding the forms in triplicate. I wanted to write, not to teach. Moreover, I had no great belief in the subject they would probably have given me, English Literature. I could never see it as an examination subject. There is something preposterous, too, about youngsters sitting down to read Keats and Shelley and calling that a week's work. They ought to be reading Keats and Shelley for fun, not for marks and credits. You can turn English Literature into a disciplined subject, but only by examining your students on a multitude of not very important facts. In my time at Cambridge, in the English Tripos, they pretended to assess your genuine powers of criticism, and hinted they were ready to throw in First Classes and Distinctions for originality and creative ability. But if Aristotle, Longinus, Coleridge, and Saint-Beuve themselves were sitting on the board of examiners, they could not keep such a rash promise. My friend and host at Boulder, who is a professor of English there, with the rare gift of being able to communicate some of his own fiery enthusiasm to his classes, told me that his trouble was that most of his students knew so little. He could not assume that they knew anything at all. If he forgot himself for a moment—not with his special picked groups, but with the general run of students—and became even mildly allusive, he was immediately sailing away above their heads. But being a genuine poet himself, he can at least give them a glimpse of the compelling creative mood. This is what students of literature are rarely offered. The average professor or lecturer on English Literature is a conscientious, dreary sort of chap, who suffers from his foolish belief that literature is something only to be found in old standard sets in the library. He never finds any in a magazine or a newspaper. He does not really know that, for better or worse, literature is still happening. He rarely has a chance to meet real writers, as distinct from fellow professors who spend the vacations of ten years writing the biography of some tepid old scribbler. Some of the best criticism in our language has been written by professors of English, but not lately, since they became teachers. The ones who wrote the good books, such as Saintsbury, Bradley, Ker, and Raleigh, were really subsidized critics, who were more interested in literature than they were in the mild little ambitions of their students. When the old professors sat up late at night it was to talk and drink, read and write; but the new lot, teachers to a man, only sit up late to mark papers or to prepare a nice little lecture or two on the Romantic Revival. That is one reason why we have so few good solid books of criticism now: the fruity old professors, who earned their pay more by writing uncommercial volumes than by lecturing, have vacated their chairs. Many of the contemporary men are products of the post-graduate thesis and Ph.D.-hunting school, and at some time or other have written their little piece about *Milton's Use of the Subjunctive, Landscape in the 18th Century Novel, The Watchman in Elizabethan Drama,* or *Three Misprints In A Shelley Pamphlet.* Write me down a traitor to scholarship and the humanities if you like, but I would prefer to see most of the public money involved here handed over to scientists, who could spend it on research that means something. No, I was not sorry I had never turned professor of English, but I felt that if I had, I probably could not have done better than to follow the example of my old friend, to have come here among these remote mountains and to have shouted my head off telling these wondering young mountaineers about the glories of English Poetry.

It was not long before my turn came to do some shouting. Roughly disguised as a distinguished scholar, I took my place in a procession that went slowly but a trifle shamefacedly—for though dons like these traditional ceremonies, they have not the soldier's knack of doing them well—into the enormous auditorium, which apparently held a waiting crowd of students and public amounting to several thousand. As we made our ponderous but highly-colored entrance, I could not help thinking about a similar ceremony in which I had taken part, eight months before, at St. Andrews. (This is a good example of the odd way in which things of a kind cluster together in life. If you break something one day, you will probably break something else the day after; and so forth. Here was I, after years away from universities, receiving two honorary degrees well within twelve months. I shall probably not have another for twenty years.) There could hardly have been a sharper contrast. The enchanting gray old Scots town looking out to sea; the little hall bright with scarlet gowns; the antique ceremony, in which a bit of stuff from John Knox's cap played its part; the solemn Scots elders and the lively lads; all under a June sun. And now this huge and terrifying auditorium seven thousand feet up somewhere among the Rocky Mountains; nothing older than the day before yesterday; the great crowd of people representing an incredible mixture of races; central heating and outside a silent iron winter. Nothing in common but a certain atmosphere of learning and teaching, and, as far as I was concerned, an equal warm friendliness.

Feeling hot and rather ridiculous, I climbed up to the platform with the others, and was put into a little chair, over which I billowed in my black gown like some enormous widow, desperately facing those thousands, who were expecting something pretty good from this new doctor of literature. An incurable childishness in me prevents my entering into the spirit of all ceremonies of this kind; I have nothing of the solemn ritualist about me, and such powers of acting as I have are comic; I could never have been a successful poli-

tician or soldier or priest; and now, as usual, I felt a
fool and longed to behave like one, to wink or grin or
pull a monstrous face. Perhaps I did, but I could only
remember sitting there, sweating and embarrassed and
rather fearful, clutching under my borrowed gown the
bundle of lecture notes, those very sheets that had now
turned up again among the litter in my hut. There had
been some music; I had been orated upon; a charming
gray and primrose silk hood had been draped over my
head; and now I was expected to entertain and instruct this formidable assembly for the rest of the afternoon. And for all my old hand's glib advice about turning
off the imagination, not being afraid of your audience, I was wabbly and dry-mouthed as I moved across
to the desk and put my notes and watch on it. "Mr.
President, Members of the Faculty . . ."

Chapter Twelve

TURNING over the notes for this Convocation Address, wondering if they were worth keeping, I saw what an odd subject I had chosen. Not that there had been anything wrong with the matter of the lecture. It had suited its purpose admirably. I had intended to cover very hastily a lot of ground, to talk to the whole university and not to one section of it, and I knew I had succeeded when, the next day at a party, professors from four or five different departments of knowledge told me that they had been discussing with their students various things I had said. If this suggests that my lecture was solidly incrusted with learning, I am deceiving you. It was not a scholarly performance at all. But it took a wide view, generalized without shame, and was equally provocative to the members of a half a dozen different schools. All that was intended. But the point of view throughout was an odd one for me to have chosen. Now that I was turning over the notes again, after a lapse of three months, I was surprised at myself. This long talk was really a plea for the inner life, the spirit. That does not sound like me at all. Among younger English writers, Charles Morgan is the official Keeper of the

Inner Life and Spiritual Department. I doubt if I should be admitted except on those days when only the more popular rooms are open. So what, in short, was I playing at? The answer is, first, that I was quite sincere, and, secondly, that the circumstances in which I had recently found myself and the nature of my own temperament had between them compelled me to deal with this particular subject.

The circumstances were that I had spent all that autumn and winter in America, often among people who seemed to me to be suffering from a poverty of the inner life, and I had recently been reading some popular works that irritated and disturbed me. And I have the kind of temperament that tends to go against the company it is keeping. It is as if my instinct is always towards restoring some lost balance. Actually I have few definite beliefs of my own, and not even the ghost of a systematic philosophy of life. Being very English, I have no contempt for compromises and am not much worried by inconsistencies. I see Man as both an intellectual and an emotional creature, and so I dislike any theory of life that treats him as being entirely one or the other. We are like ships that are more likely to reach their port if they compromise a little with wind and weather. Wisdom, I believe, will not lay a dead straight course. I do not understand either the people who will not accept the visible world at all or the people who will accept nothing else. I am equally surprised by the

[219]

persons who categorically deny God's existence and those who talk as if they knew all about Him. Each party apparently has sources of information denied to me. I distrust all immense simplications, feeling that they must be ruthlessly imposed, like the bed of Procrustes on the unhappy traveler, on the complicated patterns of reality. Truth, I believe, will be found to be shaped like a tree and not like a telegraph pole. I am not a metaphysician, but I have always been equally repelled by the idealism that denies matter and the materialism that denies mind. The scientists who sneer at religion make me feel profoundly religious. The priests who would bind and gag the scientists arouse my instant antagonism. I agree with that excellent critic, F. L. Lucas, in keeping clear of both the extreme Romantic and the extreme Classic, for "health, both in life and in literature, lies between excess of self-consciousness and excess of impulsiveness, between too much self-control and too little." Our outward life is not a mere shadow show, but neither is it the only reality. The world and our minds both exist in their own right, and we have to discover the proper relation between them. The scientist, losing himself in the world outside, forgets where he started from. The idealist philosopher or the romantic poet, burrowing deeper and deeper into himself, forgets where he is. I felt that the most satisfying life, though I was not sure I was capable of living it myself, would be a deeply symbolic one. The world, on that view, would be

neither a mischievous play of shadows and an evil dream
nor the engine in which we were cogs, but a blazingly
real heraldic display. And it was the lack of any such
feeling about it that had disturbed me.

All through this winter I had felt that things were
going from bad to worse in the world. The attempt at
collective security had failed. Hate was spreading like
a vast black cloud. More and more men would save the
world in their own way or blow it to bits. The most
devilish cruelty was now being taken for granted again.
The freedom won by centuries of effort was being given
up in an afternoon. Men were deliberately shutting and
darkening windows that their ancestors had given their
lives to open. Here in America, there was at the moment
no shadow of war. The economic machinery was straining and knocking badly and there were signs of a possible sharp conflict between the different economic classes,
but there was still a reasonable security and the people
could attend to their own affairs without feeling those
vast vibrations of fear and hate that were rocking
Europe. Yet here, too, I felt, all was not well. Somehow the people were better than the life they lived.
Most of them seemed to me bewildered and profoundly
dissatisfied, and I did not believe that more employ-
ment, higher wages, fewer taxes, though they might
help, would bring them satisfaction. Many of them
had every comfort and convenience that a wonderfully
organized material civilization could give them. Their

ordinary domestic lives would have been the envy of Persian kings and Roman Cæsars. Probably not since the world began had men and women enjoyed such an elaborate and smooth machinery of service. And yet somehow it was not working properly. People were discontented, feeling frustrated, as if they had been mysteriously cheated out of something. They rushed upon their pleasures in the hope that the sad spell would be broken. Then in the morning most of them were back again in the web of melancholy bewilderment. Some of this could be explained by the fact, which I noted earlier in this record, that the great unconscious drift of American life was rapidly moving away from the accepted official ideas of that life. But not all of it. The messy muddle of sex would explain some of it. But not all. There was something wrong with the individual's relation with the macrocosm. It was not rich and satisfying. They were wandering—indeed, we were nearly all wandering—in the wilderness between Egypt and the Promised Land. The old religion had gone out of their lives, and the new one had not yet arrived.

Looking for something to read in meagerly-stocked shops, I had bought several popular works that explained the modern world to modern man, and I had found such guides to knowledge, which were having a large sale, filled with belittling and ignoble half-truths. It seemed to me that their effect on a young and eager mind would be to dry up the springs of generous impulse.

When we despairingly wonder what is happening to the world, why people are beginning to behave as if life were worthless, we forget that for years now people have been told that this, that, and the other piece of new knowledge only removed still more of the dignity and significance of human life. This is not the fault of the scientists, who have generally the natural piety of men with a vocation. It has been the fault of their expositors, the pseudo-scientific journalists and hacks who compile these popular guides to knowledge. I was no elderly clergyman terrified of what science might do next. Nobody could be less like a Bible-thumper. I could accept with gratitude all that real science, as distinct from cheap, cocksure accounts of it, would tell me. But I found myself irritated by all this thin brittle stuff, the product of determinedly unphilosophic minds, men who had less essential wisdom than many an old fisherman or farm laborer. There were some quotations from such works among these notes, and I turned to them. Thus, a familiar example of size snobbery from a popular work on astronomy:

On this scale a plan of the whole solar system can be laid down in a field less than a mile square. Outside this field we should find a tract broader than the whole continent of America without a visible object in it unless perhaps comets scattered around its border. Far beyond the limits of the American continent we should find the nearest star, which, like our sun, might be represented by an apple. A region of the little model as large as the whole earth might contain only two or three stars. We see from this how, in a flight through the universe, like the one we have imagined, we might overlook such an insignificant little body as our earth, even if we made a careful search for it. We should be like a person flying through the Mississippi Valley looking for a grain of mustard seed which he knew was hidden somewhere on the American continent. . . .

This does very well what it first sets out to do, to show graphically the comparative physical insignificance of the earth, and we are probably all the better for realizing it, but even in this passage one cannot help feeling that some sort of depreciatory value philosophy is being cheated into the picture. And after all, a sperm whale would outbulk and outweigh scores of Einsteins. These look-at-the-size-of-the-universe fellows never use this vastness to enlarge life but always to diminish it. And this will not do. If there is life elsewhere, in higher forms than we know, then this earth remains insignificant, but the adventure of life itself broadens into a colossal epic among the stars. If there is not life elsewhere, then this earth is not insignificant but the shining centerpiece, the one great achievement, of the universe. In any event, I see no reason why we should prostrate ourselves before empty space or dead matter.

Another quotation I had used caught my eye. This time it was from a work triumphantly prophesying what science and engineering would do for us during these next hundred years. It ran:

If Life, even the very simplest form, is ever synthesized it will be a sad day for the clergy, because the implication that man is nothing more than a complicated form of laboratory product would be a little too much for even the most liberal cleric. . . .

Why? What will have produced this new synthetic life? Not the laboratory, which does not invent and erect itself and then conduct its own experiments. It will have been produced by the mind of Man in its strange and untiring pursuit of Truth. We are always being told now that "man is nothing more than a complicated form of" this and that, but the very men who tell you, after explaining that they have dedicated their lives to the proof of their particular theory, are a proof that they are wrong, that there must be something more, not contained within the formula, arriving from nowhere. I have just been looking at a large book by an American doctor, who says in his preface that he set out on his quest, forty years ago, after seeing a young man die, and made up his mind not to rest until he had proved to his own satisfaction just what it was that had happened to the young man he saw. He can now triumphantly announce that life is simply an affair of radio-electric cells, the difference between the amœba and man being that the amœba is a comparatively simple arrangement of cells, whereas man is a large and complicated one. But why this particular collection of radio-

[225]

electric cells should have spent its life on this research, it does not explain. At what stage do the cells develop a sudden selfless passion for Truth? And I know that if I were that liberal cleric, I should begin asking a few questions of this kind, and that it would not be a sad day for me at all. On the contrary; for I could then announce that my God, working through men, had moved on a stage further.

On the next sheet, there was another quotation, taken from a book with a wide sale called *Outline of Man's Knowledge*:

Jesus, as these and many other statements indicate, was a severe sufferer from what Freudians call the Œdipus Complex. He had an intense affection for his mother: the apocryphal New Testament has the angels announce that Mary will be "a holy virgin for one husband, Christ" and calls Christ "her spouse and bridegroom" constantly. Christ, in the orthodox New Testament, often called himself "the bridegroom" without naming the bride: the censor within himself or the editors of the gospels, was at work here. Moreover, his whole anarchic teaching—take no thought for the morrow, lay not up treasures upon earth, and all the impossible rest—came from the struggle against the ideas of his putative father, the hard-headed, practical-minded and practical-faithed Joseph. . . .

Now I cannot call myself a Christian, for much of the doctrine bewilders me, and some of it definitely repels, and I have long felt that it was a mistake to pile Greek philosophy and the Roman Imperial organization on top of the essentially personal teaching of this supreme religious genius. Nevertheless, the kind of hostile criticism of the Christian religion represented by the above passage fills me with despair. It is at once so terribly knowing and so terribly silly. Take it on its own ridiculous ground. An expert and hard-working psycho-analyst often has to spend months in intimate talk with a patient before he discovers the existence of an Œdipus Complex. But this writer, who is not a psycho-analyst, not expert and hard-working, discovers at once the existence of such a complex in Jesus, and proves it by quoting the metaphors of the people who wrote about him generations after his death. It is as if one of us now should write an account of John Stuart Mill and in it call him "a lover of his fellow men," and then this deep thinker should come along and on the basis of this metaphor accuse Mill of having had pederastic tendencies. We would not shoo a cat out of the room on such evidence as this, and yet he complacently hoots at one of the greatest figures in all history, some of whose words are like flashes of lightning into the inmost recesses of the human heart. And this was the knowledge that American youth, anxious to learn about this world and this life, was buying and digesting.

I was tired too of seeing, in this and similar works, the now fashionable trick of explaining a thing by its roots and not by its fruits. The writer will not say what it means to us here and now, but at once plunges blindly in the direction of its origins and begins to invent a lot of stuff about primitive men, notwithstanding the fact that he knows nothing whatever about primitive men. If, for example, his subject is immortality, he does not consider how the wisest minds have thought and felt about it, but immediately takes a jump into the pre-historical ages and tells us solemnly, as if he had been there, that primitive cavemen could at first hardly distinguish death from sleep and so left food and weapons with the dead when they themselves went out to hunt, and this explains why we seem to have an instinctive belief in survival. I had read hundreds of pages of such easy bosh, and was now impatient with its authors. Even when they were not quite so silly as this, they still cheated. When you asked for an apple, they insisted upon showing you a seed or two. When you wanted a performance of Bach's *Air on the G String*, they could not give it to you, but pretended that a tour of the violin-makers' workshops would be better for you. You left them trying to decipher a message by analyzing the paper and ink. It is not genuine scientists of repute who make these mistakes. It is the camp followers of science, the cheerfully cocksure popularizers, who thus talk old-fashioned and outmoded science, bad philosophy, and cheap irreligion all in one breath. Yet all this passed as the latest word in knowledge, and was being absorbed by hordes of youngsters only too anxious to learn. If you did not accept such knowledge, then probably you were not tough enough to take it. But they take it, feeding their bellies with the east wind, and then wonder what can be wrong with everything and why they still feel so dissatisfied. What their guides do not point out is that the poor fools who believed in the old religions, now reduced to their proper complexes, could at least make shift to answer most of the famous old riddles of this life, could look the Sphinx in the face. These guides to knowledge pretend that the Sphinx and the riddles are not there. They contemptuously dismiss in a paragraph or two the saints and philosophers of centuries, yet cannot begin to find an answer to any one of these questions, which are older than Job and yet seem new and urgent to every fresh generation. The life of humanity that we see limping out of their pages looks like a trivial accident; it is apparently unrelated to anything but primitive man and the amœba and radio-electric cells; it knows no obligations or sanctions, and is unaware of any values; it goes on complicating itself to no particular purpose; and may justly be regarded as an ignoble and futile fuss.

Considering, then, the state of the world, the bewilderment and dissatisfaction I thought I had noticed so often in America, and the belittling half-truths of these popular guides to knowledge, I had evolved this sheaf of notes for the Convocation address in Colorado.

I did not remember using them very much, except for the quotations, but I think I kept going fairly steadily along the line of their text. There are two ways of dealing with this kind of subject. You can keep yourself out of all the doubts and difficulties you report, just as if you were a philosophical social historian looking back from the year 3037. This is H. G. Wells' trick, and very impressive it is too if artfully done. It gives you an air of immense and almost godlike authority. The other way is not to pretend any detachment and superiority, to be frankly in the muddle yourself, and to be easy and personal. This suits my temperament, which has nothing of the grand and prophetic about it. I began my talk by making the not very startling announcement that I was not a profound original thinker. My qualifications for this particular task were not very remarkable. They did exist, however. My profession as novelist and dramatist made me think a good deal about real people. In our highly organized urban life of today we tended to think of people more and more as abstractions, as customers, passengers, functions, and what not, and not as real people. My profession prevented me from falling into this error. And I had been recently much impressed by the fact that, in spite of all our immense resources, people in the mass were not leading very full and happy lives.

This fact was tremendously important to me because I still believed in the supreme significance of the individual. I might be in favor of very elaborate and advanced forms of coöperation, but nevertheless I believed in the individual. I disliked the notion that the State was somehow of more importance than the sum total of the individuals in it. I made a distinction between the State and the Community. The State is really a kind of machine used by the Community, and must not be thought to possess some mystical significance. The Community must be regarded as a coöperating total of individuals. All values reside in persons. The universe expresses itself through individual minds or souls. It may have nobler forms of expression, but they are not known to us. Social insects such as bees, ants, termites, might be regarded as a terrible warning, for though in their own peculiar civilizations, which were fully developed long before ours had begun, they appear to have settled the major problems of the procreation and preservation of the species, they have paid a price that fills us with horror. "These creatures," as Maeterlinck says of the termites, "used to have wings, they have them no more. They had eyes which they surrendered. They had a sex; they have sacrificed it. . . . Compelling the sacrifice and misery of the many for the advantage or happiness of none—and all this in order that a kind of universal despair may be continued, renewed, and multiplied so long as the world shall last. . . ." They had perfected a system that had sent them swarming to the end of some awful blind alley. The very horror and instinctive revulsion with which we regarded them were perhaps significant, warning us not to go that way. However elaborate our coöperation might be, we must hold fast to the individual.

We were beginning to feel, I went on, like men who had arrived at a crossroads in the dark. There were in so many of us a deepening bewilderment, a growing fear. Which way now? There were signs that our present civilization was dangerously lopsided. Inventive man had far outreached reflective man. As Van Loon had said: "The hand is forging ahead by leaps and bounds while the brain is developing its faculties with exasperating slowness. . . . We are cave-dwellers going on a joy ride in a Chevrolet. . . ." But even our brains were not developing steadily. The world was rapidly filling with mechanical-minded persons who appeared to have little or no imagination. This lack of imagination was already having disastrous results. Science was being prostituted ruthlessly, by greedy commercialism, by lying propagandists, by all the war-mongers. It was typical of our time that whenever a new discovery was made, its possibility as a destructive force or weapon was immediately emphasized. The airplane, which ought to have been the ally of civilization, had almost become a symbol of terrible destruction. It was looking as if man had only taken to the air to indulge in indiscriminate slaughter. We were like children who had been given razors to play with. The rapid transport and lightning communications of our time only seemed to reveal our fundamental poverty. We could paraphrase Matthew Arnold's famous question, and ask what was the use of air services and express trains and giant liners if they only took us from a dismal and illiberal life in Europe to a dismal and illiberal life in America. We seemed to be in danger of producing a race of passive-minded, robot-like people, with no initiative, no genuine appetites, no free intelligence, helpless victims of all the forces of publicity. Many of our apparent victories might be defeats. A great deal of cheap mass production, for example, might be doing far more harm to the people engaged in it than any possible good it might be doing to the rest of the public. There were signs of a widening lack of zest, intellectual marrow, downright character. And unfortunately this civilization of ours was now dominating the world. Thus, in China and Japan, it had driven out forms of civilization that had endured, sometimes very fruitfully, for ages. In the earlier history of the world, it had been always possible to make various experiments in social life, but now everybody everywhere appeared to be moving in the same direction. This left us with a terrific responsibility. If we blundered into another dark age, it would cover the whole world.

At the gloomy crossroads where we appeared to be standing, we could catch a glimpse of several different roads, each with its hopeful signpost. The first might be called optimistic scientific materialism. I had just read several books praising this route and promising wonders at the end of it. Their authors believed that what we needed most were more and more things, and that if we gave the chemists and the engineers our enthusiastic support they would soon produce a magical abundance of these things. Soon we should all be happy in a world crammed with safety razors, toothbrushes, shower baths, television sets, autogyros, glass houses, and synthetic rubber highways. I said that these things were worth having and so worth trying for, although I could not forget the small ironical fact that while my father had effectively used one razor, an old *Hamburg Ring,* all his life, somehow I had been compelled to use dozens with less efficiency, and that I could not quite see how I was better off. But I did not believe that this was a way out. At the best, it could only help to find a way out. We cannot seek grace through gadgets. We can be just as unhappy in spun-glass trousers as we were in worsted ones. In a bakelite house the dishes may not break, but the heart can. Even a man with ten shower-baths can still find life stale, flat, and unprofitable. This solution only satisfied the men who put it forward because they saw themselves on the active side and not the passive side of this business, knew that they would be happy enough among the innumerable laboratories and workshops. Such a world as they prophesy for us is merely an expression of their own temperaments. And how easily they give themselves away! I quoted one revealing sentence from a very popular specimen of this optimistic scientific materialism: "There must be musicians, writers, and artists who put the trimmings on life." By that one simple statement the author shows us quite plainly that he has not the least idea, has never had and probably never will have the least idea of what musicians and writers and artists hope to do, try to do, and frequently succeed in doing. A Zulu or Eskimo would know better than that. Trimmings indeed!

Another suggested way out was through pseudo-mystical and militant nationalism. This offered us the rather droll spectacle of Germany fervently worshiping Germany. To join this cult, you had first to banish reason. But the fact that this nonsense could exist and be successful was itself a proof of the failure of our civilization. People took to such cults not only for political and economic reasons, but because they found something satisfying about their immense emotional demands and supplies. It was as if, from walking idly about the streets, they were suddenly taken into the blood-and-sawdust atmosphere of a gladiatorial circus. The point is, they had to have *something* that made life seem rich and significant. I saw it myself as neurotic and leading to a new barbarism. I had far more sympathy with the next way out, labeled Marx. Here at least there was often a genuine passion for social justice. But it seemed

[235]

to me that the orthodox Communist found himself on a hopelessly narrow basis for real living. He was like a man who had invented some sort of gruel and would have nothing else for breakfast, dinner and supper. Communism, if successful, was liable to fall into the error of optimistic scientific materialism, just as we saw how Russia was busy imitating America. When every citizen has a car and a radio, we shall not have automatically entered the Kingdom of Heaven. And indeed, if the car can only take us from one group of factories to another, and the radio only tell us how good the State is to us, we might be better off without either of them. We must remember that on these lines the bees and ants have done very well for themselves, but that we do not envy them. I admitted that I was not intimately acquainted with the philosophy of Marx and Lenin, but from the little I did know of it, I thought it seemed to leave too many important matters unexplained. The philosophy of Marx and Lenin did not seem to me to explain Marx and Lenin. I could not see how two such beings, who braved everything for what they believed to be the truth, had been produced by the dialectical material processes of this world.

I went on to say that though political and economic matters were extremely important, I could not help feeling that the operation of their laws did not explain all modern evils. There was probably something wrong with our individual relation to life, something that explained our very feeble desire for peace, the growing intolerance and violence in the world, the restless, uncreative search for pleasure, the lack of real happiness. In the last resort, much could be accounted for by the poverty and emptiness of our inner lives. The passionate interest in crime as well as our continued concern with war bore witness to a numbed sensibility and a lack of imagination. There was no longer a widespread feeling of purpose and grandeur in life. I was no enemy of material progress, and believed that the social conscience that urged us to extend the benefits of our material civilization was an essential part of our spiritual life. I was certainly no enemy of popular amusements, for I had often contributed to them and often defended them. They needed defense, I thought, because many intellectuals wrongly attacked them, sometimes showing far less wisdom and sensitiveness than the ordinary man. (For example, about films, before they suddenly became a highbrow fashion.) But it was time we found more riches in ourselves. Sometimes we should think of Man as an instrument himself and not merely as a maker of instruments. The East could teach us something here. It was possible that much valuable knowledge was in danger of being lost, simply because it did not conform to our now fashionable standards. We ought to keep alive that poetic wonder which all great scientists seem to possess in good measure and which seems to be unknown to their drum-beating followers.

But we should combine with it a truly critical and philosophical spirit. Man is a metaphysical as well as a political animal. We were now in a stage of almost universal half-education, and many of our dangers and weaknesses come from this fine experiment. The shrewdness of mind and essential richness of life often known to illiterate craftsmen had been lost. Here I brought in my quotations from and criticisms of those guides to knowledge. I pointed out that the so-called scientific attitude of the writers of these works was already looking too rigid and old-fashioned. The mechanistic universe was melting away. Science must go on and on, but that does not mean that nothing else must go with it. Comte had once suggested a division of our history into religious, metaphysical, and scientific eras, but it might be that there was a circular or, better still, a spiral movement, and that we might be approaching a new metaphysical era that would develop into a new religious age.

Here there were a few pages of these notes missing and I did not trouble to find them. The next and last page but one said in my boldest print hand, "Mystery of Time." I remembered then that I had concluded by saying that we might be close to one of these great revelations that suddenly enlarge and enrich our vision of life. We were, I felt, due for one. And I believed that this revelation might explode, once and for all, the bewildering problem of Time. No sooner had I remembered saying that than I was no longer still talking in that enormous auditorium among the Rockies. I forgot Colorado and remembered California, for it was when we had gone to Santa Barbara and then from there to Death Valley that I had found myself caught in the coils of this Time problem. Remembering these places and that maze of speculation, I left the table, at which I had been reading my Colorado notes, sat down again and lit another pipe, to try in comfort to recall what I had seen and thought and felt during those weeks.

Chapter Thirteen

WE HAD gone to Hollywood again, and on the very second day I felt I did not want to stay in the place another night longer, so I hastily concluded my business there, and we motored up the queer higgle-piggledy coast to Santa Barbara. Here the oil wells, whose pumps and steel lattice work stand in the sea like wading Martians, suddenly come to an end, and a great deal of old Mexican charm is turned on, probably because the people who used to make their millions out of the oil decided to live near Santa Barbara. Some of the town, however, does date from the eighteenth century, and the famous Mission is very charming. The Pacific tumbles and roars at the foot of the town, and immediately behind it are mountains that look more like real mountains, and less like shabby brown skin-rugs, than those near Los Angeles. Everything in the place is determinedly picturesque. After allowing for the fact that it is rather artificial and arty, parasitic, a private-income sort of town, you must grant it most of the charm it boasts about. It is all still faintly unreal, but not so unreal as Hollywood and Beverly Hills. There was an odd salty lushness about it that pleased me. I could smell the sea, and smell the flowers and leaves, which is more than I could do further south.

We did not stay in Santa Barbara itself, but a mile or two out, at the Biltmore Hotel on Montecito Beach. I liked this hotel so much that when my family went to find the Rainbow Bridge up in Utah and I could not go with them because I had some work to finish, I returned here. It is newish and very well designed, a long low Spanish type of building, with red pantile roofs and cream walls, plenty of trees, including huge palms, and fine lawns that run to the sea's edge. A very luscious job. I lived in the patio, in a room with a little balcony overlooking bright beds of snapdragon and cineraria and the fruit and blossom of orange trees. A macaw, colored like a pirate captain, squawked among the leaves. Outside there were cypresses and eucalyptus trees among the tall palms. The air was heavy and sweet with the scent of flowers lingering in the faint sea mists. It was all what the tropics ought to be and somehow never are. Tennyson ought to have come here to write his "Lotus Eaters." But perhaps the whole place, palms and surf and all, had been designed out of Tennyson, and perhaps one of its former millionaires had installed an apparatus somewhere for scenting the air. I liked it, and would return to it with pleasure, but I never quite freed my mind of the suspicion that there was something a trifle synthetic about it all. There was nothing madly luxurious about the hotel itself; but it was solidly com-

[241]

fortable as well as picturesque; and when I was not smoking on my balcony, pretending to work, or was not outside staring at the Pacific across the lawns, I could take some violent exercise playing the pro at lawn tennis, at which I sweated gloriously in that moist air. But even this did not break the odd drowsy spell of the place. I used to go to and from my patio in a kind of long dream.

In the center of the town is a reconditioned huddle of old Spanish buildings, with an amusing Mexican restaurant in the middle of them, called "El Paseo," and here I found, among other quaint establishments, an excellent little bookshop, kept by an American who wants to retire one day to the Cotswolds, having had his share now of Californian charm. In this bookshop, a familiar minor miracle happened. I am not a man of destiny; I follow no star; no angelic voices guide me; I live, like the majority, in an earthy muddle. Except in one small particular. If I begin thinking about a book that I do not possess, a book that is out of print or not easily accessible, that book will shortly turn up, often in a most unlikely place. This has happened to me over and over again; and if it is Chance, then Chance is bookish and biased in my favor. Now for some weeks before going to Santa Barbara I had been wanting to lay my hands on a strange work by Ouspensky, the Russian mathematician and mystic, called *A New Model of the Universe.* I had seen it referred to several times, but knew very little about it. I did not believe that it had ever been published in England, and if these references were to an American edition, I did not know who was the publisher. So I did nothing about it. But I had not been two minutes in this little bookshop in "El Paseo," Santa Barbara, before I noticed in the corner of a low shelf a copy of *A New Model of the Universe*, a solitary copy that had been there several years and that the proprietor was only too delighted to sell to me. Chance again, no doubt; though there was no book I was more anxious to find than this, and it was at least twenty to one against my finding it in a shop of this size. I had not even been looking for it when I did find it. You may retort that this was precisely the kind of mystical-magical work that a Santa Barbara bookseller, with a few rich old theosophical ladies to cater for, would have in stock. But if so, why hadn't he sold it, why had it been there so long waiting for me? I returned to my little balcony above the patio, peeping into the volume as I went. Here was a place that for all its color and fragrance, its tall palms and thundering ocean, was somehow so thin, brittle, and dreamlike that it hardly seemed to have three dimensions, and now here was P. D. Ouspensky, ready to tell me all about the fourth dimension and even prepared to make a few observations about the fifth and sixth dimensions. Now this, I said to myself, is the stuff to give 'em.

Throughout this winter I had played with the idea

of following my novel with a little book on Time. My qualifications for writing such a book were magnificently inadequate. I know just enough philosophy to know how little I know, and I am as practiced in mathematical reasoning as a Hottentot. No, I had no illusions about my ability to instruct other people on such a theme. All I could bring to it was my professional trick of rather easy and pleasant exposition. But I wanted to write the little book for my own sake, to see what would happen to me in that dark forest of speculation. I knew that however fascinated I might be by the problem of Time, no matter how many hours I might spend reading everything I came across on the subject, I would give no real hard thought to it until I had to turn my thinking into paragraphs and chapters. For several years I had had a hunch—I dare not call it anything better —that this problem of Time was the particular riddle that the Sphinx has set for this age of ours, that it was like a great barrier across our way and we were all squabbling and shouting and moaning in its shadow, and that if it could be solved there might follow a wonderful release and expansion of the human spirit. Even in the most fantastic of my pipe dreams, I had never imagined that any little book by me would help to bring about this renaissance. I hoped—and am still hoping— that somewhere there was an unknown speculative genius, "voyaging on strange seas of thought, alone," who would soon arrive with the News. I knew only too well that I had not the training, the patience, the right kind of mind. Sometimes I felt rather like a man who can play about three notes on the violin and discovers the score of a colossal unknown concerto, so that he looks at the bewilderingly rich pages and now and then uncertainly twangs a string or dubiously gropes for his bow. And I also felt very much alone in my curiosity. I never seemed to run across many real philosophers, and all the other people I knew well, though their range of interest was as wide as the world, from goosanders to Gregorian chants, failed to light up when I told them I could not understand this Time business. Apparently it was all plain and dull sailing to them. Time went on and on and on, you couldn't stop it, and that was that. They were blankly incurious. But they did not shake my belief that if we could find a key to fit this lock we might open a door into a new universe. And we could do with a new universe.

The wildest theory of fantastic dimensions seemed to me to have a little more sense in it than the conventional view of Time, which nearly everybody I knew accepted without question. According to this account of the matter, all that really exists is the present moment, Now. The Past, the real Past and not the memory traces of it in the brain, has vanished. Yesterday is with the ages, and they have all gone to Limbo. The Future has not arrived. It cannot be said to have any shape, any quality; it is nothing, like the Past. Between these two nothings is a razor edge of actuality, the present moment, the Now. This Now apparently endures for us for about a tenth part of a second. In that tenth part of a second we have all our life. One blink and it has gone, taking the whole universe with it. Another blink and a new universe has arrived, an instantaneous creation, only to be destroyed as soon as we have shouted "Now!" We cannot even be said to be moving steadily from nothing to nothing. Who are we? Yet all our metaphors about Time—and metaphors that are in fashion for thousands of years are worth considering as evidence —speak of it in terms of movement. They do not even hint that Time is busy destroying and creating the world every fraction of a second. These metaphors tell us that Time is carrying us along, a stream, a chariot, a river. We are told that we have an intuitive perception of this movement. If we are knocked unconscious, we realize at once, on returning to consciousness that there has been a lapse of Time, that the ever-rolling stream has carried us a little farther. But this movement suggests a background that is not moving. The stream flows between apparently motionless banks. If Time flows like a universal stream, what is it that does not move, where are its banks? How do we know that we are moving on and on? And why do we say that now Time flies, now it crawls. If the clock is measuring Time for us, where is the clock we consult when we say that the ordinary clock is flying or crawling? How

could this conventional Time be single and universal?
I had never been able to make any sense of it.

Years ago I had read a little work that seemed to me
to confirm some vague speculations of my own. It was
called *Flatland: A Romance of Many Dimensions*, was
published in 1884 at half a crown, has long been out of
print and rather hard to find. (Somebody ought to re-
publish it.) It describes, with quiet donnish irony, the
life of the inhabitants of Flatland, who are beings who
appear to themselves to exist on a two-dimensional plane
and who are therefore geometrical shapes, without thickness. The narrator, a member of the professional class,
is a Square. He is visited by a very disturbing stranger,
who has the power of changing his shape and of
appearing and disappearing in Flatland at will, and
this stranger, who is actually a sphere and therefore
three-dimensional, tells our friend Square, that there
exists a world of three dimensions. The doubting Square
is finally shown a vision of this fantastic world of
three dimensions, which seems to him very strange but
of amazing beauty and vitality. Afterwards he tries to
teach the truth of three dimensions to his fellow Flat-
landers, who promptly put him in prison. Now you can,
if you like, take this as a piece of charming geometrical
fooling, probably written to amuse a small university set.
That is what it must have seemed to be fifty years ago,
and I imagine that very few people even today would
see any real significance in its antics with dimensions.

People in general are not interested in dimensions. They have not realized yet that out of this seemingly wild or idle talk about them there may come discoveries and beliefs that will change the whole universe for us. The author of *Flatland* quietly proceeds by way of analogy. The two-dimensional creature is bewildered by the three-dimensional one, who has the power of moving in a new and inconceivable direction, and also the power of seeing everything that is happening in Flatland because he has only to look down on its two-dimensional plane to possess all its secrets. There was some excuse in the 'eighties for anybody who thought this analogy merely fanciful. But a great deal has happened since then. Mathematicians and physicists, working at their figures without a glimmer of humorous fancy, have been compelled to assume the existence of a fourth dimension, to say nothing of a fifth or sixth. We are told, for example, that you cannot begin to fit the electron into a three-dimensional world. It has even been said that the encounter of two electrons demands a six-dimensional universe for them to meet in. This means that we can reasonably press the analogy of Flatland and Spaceland. We can read with sympathy the account of the Flatlander who suddenly found himself in Spaceland, because lately we have begun to see ourselves as Spacelanders who have been granted a vision of Space-Timeland. We are beings with a three-dimensional

[248]

outlook who are called upon to make sense out of a fourth dimension.

Now, oddly enough, although I have not a mathematical mind, I had thought about these dimensions even before I had read *Flatland* and long before I had read Hinton and Dunne and Ouspensky. One thing I had discovered for myself. It is something that is not made clear by the author of *Flatland*. Let us return to these two-dimensional beings, and assume that although their outlook is severely two-dimensional, knowing only length and breadth, they are actually living in a three-dimensional world, which has thickness too. They will see everything in terms of flat geometrical shapes. Thus, a pyramid passing through the two-dimensional plane of their consciousness would appear as a succession of triangles dwindling to a point. A sphere would arrive as a mere point and then produce a succession of growing circles until its full diameter was reached. I saw then that to such beings the third dimension could only appear in successive states, running in a before-and-after direction, quite unlike the other two dimensions, and therefore not in Space but in Time. What is obvious to us three-dimensional beings as mere thickness would seem to them so much growth or decay in Time. Our account of a sphere that could be seen all at once in three dimensions, a sphere with all its parts co-existent, would seem to them fantastic, mystical. Their sturdy common sense would reject such wild talk. Having arrived so far by myself, there was nothing absurd to me in the notion that we might be creatures with a three-dimensional outlook living in a four-dimensional world, and being compelled to regard the shape of things along their fourth dimension as a series of changes in Time. I could understand, though not very clearly, perhaps, that what we call Time—or part of what we call Time—might be simply our mode of apprehending a fourth dimension. We have taught ourselves—for it is doubtful if animals, very young children, and perhaps very primitive adults see things quite in this fashion—to perceive length and breadth and thickness, but the remaining dimension at right angles to them enters our consciousness as a series of changes. It is as if the focus of our attention had to move itself along the line of this fourth dimension, like a glowworm slowly moving over the face of a great statue. In other words, we never see things as they really are, but see a series of three-dimensional cross-sections of them. Our minds cannot conceive the other dimension except as movement, change, the flow of Time. So much I had worked out for myself, some years ago, and I was always looking for some sort of confirmation of this very rough-and-ready bit of speculation. And I have never had long to wait. Perhaps that is why I have felt that this problem of Time was our own special problem, the particular Sphinx's riddle for this age. The mysterious great current of thought, which carries on its slow drift the minds of scientists and philosophers and artists, seemed to be moving in this direction. Perhaps we might all wake up one morning to discover that we had landed on a new shore.

Since then I had both read and listened to J. W. Dunne, that hard-headed aeronautical inventor who had suddenly exploded a philosophical bombshell by publishing his first book, *An Experiment with Time.* I had happened to be among its reviewers. Although no man tries harder to be clear and concise in his expression than Dunne does, his thought is not always easy to follow, especially by a reader like myself with no mathematical training. But unlike most general readers, who were instantly attracted by his theory of dreams and then skipped the rest, I was far more interested in his philosophy itself, which he calls *Serialism,* than I was in his theory of dreams, which served as an introduction to the philosophy. It hooked my imagination at once because it concentrated upon my two favorite puzzles, that of self-consciousness and that of Time. There had always been something bewildering to me about the idea of self-consciousness. We observe something, and we are conscious of our observation, and we are conscious of the observation of the observation, and so forth. I had always felt that science could have nothing final to say about this, because no matter how science approaches life, something is always left out of the explanation of what science sees, because there is always

[251]

something in the scientist himself that is standing outside the world he is considering. There was the same mysterious confusion about Time. Something was timing the movement of what we call Time, and there was another Time beyond that to time the timing, and so forth. Dunne's explanation is that both self-consciousness and Time are regressive series, that is, series beginning with a unique first term, and then going off into infinity with all their terms in identical relations with each other. Dunne's favorite illustration, I remembered, was that of a family: the first term of the regress is a male child, who is a son but not yet a father; the second term is his father, who is both a father and a son; the third term is the grandfather, who is also both a father and a son; and so on. The basis of his argument was that reality cannot be understood except as a regression. If he is wrong in thinking that, if his regressive series do not really mean anything, then his whole philosophy collapses.

I had been told that he had been neatly refuted by some professional logician, but I had not seen the refutation. Also, I had been bewildered all my thinking life by these two riddles, self-consciousness and Time, and none of the clever professionals had helped me much. Dunne's theory did at least make straight for the biggest obstacles. He believes that each of us is a series of observers existing in a series of Times. To Observer One, our ordinary fully-awake sharp selves, the fourth dimension appears as Time. To Observer Two, which is the self we know in dreams when the first observer is not functioning, the fifth dimension would appear as Time. This second observer has a four-dimensional outlook, and this fact explains the fantastic scenery and action characteristic of dreams, in which everything seems to be so fluid, incidents have no proper beginning or ending, houses melt into woods. Dunne says this is because we try to interpret in our ordinary three-dimensional fashion these strange images gathered by our four-dimensional selves, who have to work during sleep without the sharp focus and business-like attention of the first observer. Remembering dreams on waking, we feel as if we had been plunged into another kind of existence, and tend to laugh at them though there is often lingering in our minds a feeling that somehow they were oddly significant. This is at the base of that familiar scene of the breakfast table, the late dreamer trying to convey the quality of his dream to listeners who cannot help feeling—and usually looking—very bored. Now Dunne holds that the dreaming self, now moving Time Two, has a wide length of Time One, the fourth dimension, stretched before it, and so contrives to telescope into the fantastic narratives of dream both images from the Past and *images from the Future*. It was this interpretation of dreams, forced upon him by his own experience, that opened these dizzy vistas to Dunne. Over a period of years, he remembered and

[253]

analyzed many of his dreams, made elaborate notes, and then discovered that they ransacked the Future as well as the Past. You dream, we will say, that you see three elephants walking round and round a pond. On waking you remember that the pond is one you knew as a child. But you have never seen three elephants walking in that particular fashion. Yet perhaps, years hence, you will one day see these three elephants, not walking round a pond, but moving in the same way as they did in your dream. You arrive, you see, at that point in the track of Time One which you as Observer Two, to whom Time One is not real time, caught a glimpse of, years before, in the dream. And when and if you do see the elephants, you will then be troubled by that strange haunted feeling of familiarity, of having seen all this before, which so often puzzles us. There are several different explanations of this queer but universal experience, ranging from reincarnation to a supposed occasional time lag between the two halves of the brain, but Dunne's had always seemed to me not only the most fascinating, but also the most satisfying. And his theory of dreams went farther than all others in accounting for the queer scenery and personages and action of these dramas of the night.

Out of this Serialism of Dunne's came a theory of immortality that does escape most of the criticism that seems to us to destroy the older theories. Their weakness is that they assume that the conventional view of

Time as single and universal is the true one. Jones, as a ghost, a soul awaiting the final judgment, a spirit among the loquacious Red Indians who join in seances, just goes on and on and on. And the opponents of immortality have always triumphantly asked: "Which Jones goes on? Why should the old Jones of the deathbed go on, when the boy Jones, the young man Jones, the Jones in his prime, have already perished?" And Jones himself, perhaps already feeling tired and old, does not want this immortality. Better to sink into eternal sleep than to endure, apparently forever, any of these rum existences beyond the grave. The biologist, seeing Jones as one member out of the innumerable members of one species out of the innumerable species, asks why this creature should expect to survive forever. The only immortality he can expect is what Wells calls "merger-immortality." It is the race that survives, and Jones had better try and identify himself with the higher manifestations of the race. What is strictly individual in us is not worth more than the sixty or seventy years it receives. Life is eternal, but not Jones, who is only a temporary phenomenon. The argument and the attitude of mind are very familiar. The conclusions are correct if Time is single and universal. On that level of Time that gives us dates for the calendar, Jones is most certainly mortal. He will die and disappear just as once he was born and appeared. The final exit is as certain as the first entrance. When the scientist, speaking *qua* scientist, says that immortality is an absurdity to him, he is being quite reasonable, because in the single-time world in which science goes to work, immortality must be impossible. How can Jones live on and on in it? Does he get older and older? A nightmare. Does he stay at one age? An impossibility. Does he suddenly grow younger? Preposterous. If in trying to reply to this, we mutter something about Jones having a soul, the scientist very naturally replies, in his official capacity, that he cannot find a place in Jones for the soul. It is true that soon he may have to enlarge Jones considerably.

This winter I had read and heard some accounts of the long series of tests made by Professor Rhine and his assistants at Duke University. Working with scientific detachment and accuracy and making hundreds of thousands of tests, Professor Rhine had apparently definitely established the fact that the powers of clairvoyance and telepathy exist and are not even very rare. They are extrasensory powers, cannot be explained by any known form of radiation, seem to be indifferent to distance and to penetrate all barriers. They have no right to exist, but it has been handsomely proved now that they do. So even in the simplified single-time world of science, Jones is still a mysterious fellow. But in that world he will certainly die and disappear, and when his time comes, he may not be sorry to go. But the very phrase, so old, so familiar, "his time," is significant.

If Time is illusory, or multiple, our mode of apprehending a dimension of things that we cannot grasp spatially, then there is nothing absurd or contradictory about Jones' immortality. The question, "Which Jones?" can now be answered. The answer is, Jones, the whole Jones, the Jones of the cradle, the schoolroom, the office, the mansion, the nursing home, the complete fourth-dimensional length of Jones. And this is obviously the real Jones. When we think of persons with whose lives we are fairly familiar, we always tend to take this fourth-dimensional view of them. If you say "Napoleon" to me, I have a confused instantaneous vision of many different three-dimensional figures, the boy in Corsica, the lean young artillery officer, the stout emperor, the dying man at St. Helena, various cross-sections of the four-dimensional reality that was Napoleon. Again, Jones having completed the movement along his fourth-dimensional track, coming to the end of it in death, is not a disembodied creature wistfully keeping up with the rest of us, but may now move at right angles to our direction in what appears to him to be a new Time, taking the length of his four-dimensional self along a fifth dimension. This sounds anything but simple, but there is not much evidence in support of simplicity in the universe. Nor is it completely unimaginable, for, according to Dunne, we catch a confused glimpse, immensely confused and chaotic because we try to interpret what we experience in terms that lack a necessary dimension, of this more complicated existence in our dreams. As a series of observers with our attention forever moving across new fields of Time that are really added dimensions, we must in Dunne's view, be immortal, or, at least, the ultimate observer in us must be immortal. We are engaged, according to him, in the process of learning how to live. On this theory, the tragic brevity of life is immeasurably expanded and is no longer tragic. Most of us have often felt that there is something dreadfully, pitifully extemporary about our lives, which are so much a hand-to-mouth muddle, a jumble of poor speeches and paltry gestures, with full awareness and wisdom always arriving too late. We seem like speakers or singers hurried on to a platform without preparation. There is more than sheer greed of experience in our hunger for immortality. There is something nobler than mere fear of death. We cannot help feeling that life is worth more than the sketchy improvisation we have given it. We are like actors who regret they did not make more of a part.

Now Dunne's theory not only suggests this immense enlarging of experience and opportunity, but gives some account of the process of our education. As the three-dimensional Observer One, in Time One, we use the physical brain, which must perish when our Time One comes to an end. But that brain, with its sharp focus of attention, has been teaching the mind to think. We are not lofty beings who have descended for a period into the flesh. Dunne believes that immortal mind is less mature and in more need of instruction than that mortal instrument, the brain. On this view, our flesh-and-blood Time One life serves as a sort of apprenticeship to these more complicated existences in unknown times and dimensions. There is, however, no conventional passing from one life to another, because we exist from the first as a series of observers in a series of times. The difference between one existence and the next, I take it, would be that what appeared to be Time to one would be seen as a dimension by the next, that the sharp focus of attention would pass from Observer One dealing with Time One, to Observer Two dealing with Time Two, and so on. There have always seemed to me many baffling complications in the machinery of this progress, but it does suggest a universe of the right size, complexity, richness. Unfortunately, Dunne has not, I imagine, the kind of temperament that would encourage him to enlarge on the philosophic, ethical, æsthetic, religious implications of his theory. In his second book, which I had read the summer before I sailed for New York, he had attempted to prove that the dilemmas and anomalies of modern physics were the result of the scientific treatment of Time as absolute instead of regressive. Physics, with its confusion of waves and particles, had now reached a point at which its view of Time clouded its sight. Whether he succeeded or not, I did not know, and I suspected that very few other people knew, either. He was badly situated in this second book. His nonscientific readers could not follow his juggling with waves and particles and *quanta* and relativity, and the scientific ones would retreat in horror from his theory of the Immortal Observer. I could only hope that he was at work again on a third volume, broader in its outlook, and had not decided that he had already told a noisy, wrangling, idiotic world more than it deserved to know.

Though I had a suspicion that Dunne might have gone wrong in the elaboration of his theory, with the endlessly reflected mirrors of his regressive series, I had come to believe that his view of Time must be somewhere near the truth. We were existing in more times than one. We were far more complicated beings than had been generally supposed. The Flatlander had been amazed by the power of the Spacelander who, moving up and down freely, could penetrate all the secrets of Flatland. We were Spacelanders who were just beginning to be amazed by what the Space-Timelanders, moving freely along the fourth dimension, might be able to do, and perhaps were doing. The creative imagination might be a kind of traveler's ticket for a certain amount of journeying along this dimension. I remembered then having run into William Gerhardi very late one night, the summer before, and having listened to his theory that true art is a fourth dimensional account of things. His idea was that you have to free your mind from the domination of Time to see life properly, and that once you can do that, as soon as you have turned Time into a dimension, everything takes on a curious beauty. He meant, I think, what Proust meant. To Proust it was not the initial experience that had value, but the involuntary recapturing of the experience in memory. The recaptured experience seemed to exist magnificently for its own sake. It had now a flavor and color and fragrance that it had not before, when it was being lived, not because it was seen in memory through a sentimental haze, but because now that Time was no longer hurrying it away, it could be seen and explored for its own sake. It was as if now that Time had stopped roaring in our ears, we could listen to the music of our experience. This was what Gerhardi was saying when he insisted upon the fourth dimensional view. The scene was no longer blurred or streaming away from us or broken by the beat of our anxious hearts. Passionate lovers who meet rarely and then only for short periods find they have not time to be happy, they are too conscious of the flying minutes. But in an interior by Vermeer, the room and the people in it all seem to be secure and smiling in eternity. In spite of their dark confusion, our dreams have moments of this shining peace. Mere duration does not do the trick. It is not that but our freedom from the ticking tyranny of Time that suddenly gives things this exquisite rounded quality. That rich involuntary memory which Proust makes the basis of his gigantic novel gives us a certain freedom along the line of the fourth dimension, and it is significant that in Proust's novel the ordinary Time values are almost as confused as they seem to be in a dream. The hero and his friends seem to be all ages; there is no steady progress through the calendar; Time hardly appears in its familiar guise; and yet how exquisitely and movingly a whole lost world is recreated. There is much there, of course, that belongs to the temperament of an oddly perverse invalid. But the originality and the real significance of the work had always seemed to me to come from the novelist's deliberate escape from Time's one-way track, and from his curious four-dimensional picture of his world and his characters. *A La Recherche du Temps Perdu.* He found that nothing had been lost. It was all there, waiting for him.

On this view of time, the Past has not vanished like a pricked bubble. To understand this dimension of things we move in Time as a blind man's finger moves over a piece of carving. Our consciousness travels along this track as we might travel on a railway journey. Then the Past is the station we have just left, and the Future is the station we are approaching. The Past has not been destroyed any more than the last station was destroyed when the train left it. Just as the station is still there, with its porters and ticket inspectors and bookstall and its noise and bustle, so the Past still exists, not as a dim memory, but in all its color and hum. Somewhere back along that fourth dimensional track of the world, the

[262]

dinosaurs are still roving, the ice age is melting, men are building the Pyramids and Babylon, Cæsar is being assassinated, Shakespeare is just finishing *Hamlet*, and Lincoln is making his Gettysburg speech. Nothing—not a syllable, not the wink of an eyelash—has been lost. Alexander and his men are still marching to India; Columbus is crossing the Atlantic; Old St. Paul's is blazing in the Great Fire; Mrs. Siddons is playing Lady Macbeth; and Beethoven is conducting the *Eroica*.

The three-dimensional aspect of the world is formidable enough, but its four-dimensional aspect must be terrific. All its Past is in existence along this track, not as a ghostly memory, a shadow show, but solidly real in its own eternal Present. This thought frees us from a familiar nightmare, more familiar to us than to our ancestors. For we are often told that whether men go on murdering each other or succeed at last in building up a genuine world civilization, it will all be the same in the end. The sun will cool, the planets will freeze, all life will vanish. Man and all his works must go on forever. The longer the view—as, for example, in Olaf Stapledon's strange prose epic *Last and First Men*—the deeper the feeling of tragic futility. Death has the last word. Oblivion creeps steadily nearer. But this is only true if you believe in the absolute reality of what we call Time. If the Past exists, then the end of the world is only like the end of a novel or a play, a sort of necessary artistic device. We do not find anything futile or tragic in the fact that the earth is not three dimensionally infinite and immeasurable. It has to have a shape. It must have a fourth-dimensional shape, too. When it comes to the end of its fourth-dimensional track, the whole history of the world, whatever men have done, will then be completed. No more can be added to it. But it will all be there, alive and kicking, in its own Time. And this belief, unlike so much contemporary thought, does not reduce our actions to the futile buzzing of a fly, but vastly increases the significance of our lives. We may be doing two things in this life: playing a part in the ever-enduring Time One drama of the world; and shaping our fourth dimensional body, perhaps assembling the raw material—the scenery and properties and characters of the drama—to be used in future lives. When the whole Jones finds himself in a new Time, which is really his movement along the fifth dimension, he may discover that he is very awkwardly saddled with all his Time One experience. We cannot be sent to heaven or hell, but perhaps we can build them for ourselves.

If the Past exists, however, then what about the Future? Dunne maintains, with some show of evidence, that we catch glimpses of it in our dreams. It is already there, then, waiting for us to arrive at it. How can we then, as Bergson hopefully insisted, create the Future? I pick up a pencil and while holding it I feel that I can please myself whether I put it down again or fling it across the room. There are two possible and different Futures, one with the pencil back on the table and one with the pencil lying on the floor. But on this view of Time, with the shape of things along one dimension merely experienced successively, the pencil was already either back on the table or lying on the floor, and my feeling that I had some choice in the matter was entirely illusory. I remembered that Dunne had written about "intervention," and I had a confused recollection of his arguing that if, for example, I did not want to meet the three elephants I had seen in my dream, one of my observers could "intervene" to prevent my meeting them. But if this was so, what became of the elephants that my Observer Two had seen at some point in my Time One? How did I manage to remove the elephants from the Time track or alternatively quit the track before I met the elephants? I had always felt in the old heated discussions of Free Will and Determination that no solution was possible because in some way we could not arrive at the right basis of discussion: we had no key to fit this particular lock. But here was the good old problem turning up in an even more complicated form. We felt free to choose, yet not only had our choice been determined for us, but all the multitudinous consequences of it had been settled. And if my life was not a voyage on the universal stream of Time, but simply the discovery of the fourth-dimensional contour of things, then what or who had determined the shape

[265]

of that contour? How did those three elephants arrive in my Time One? How had my Future been arranged or designed for me? In theory, I could not hold that I had anything to do with it, just as I do not feel that I am responsible for the three-dimensional measurements of my head. Yet in practice I felt that I had a good deal of responsibility about the Future. It seemed to me that not a little of what was happening to me this year was the result of what I had decided to do last year. I was back in the old maze. Had Ouspensky a plan of this maze? Could he lead me out?

I read most of his *New Model of the Universe* in Death Valley. This is a simple autobiographical fact, not a bit of romantic symbolism. We fled from Santa Barbara because quite suddenly the whole dreamy sun-lit panorama of palm and orange trees and snapdragon vanished, the sky rushed down upon us, then opened to let out a cataract of rain. We had not come halfway across the world to be drenched. If we wanted rain, there was sweeter rain than this in England. We piled our things and ourselves into the car and went roaring and splashing towards the desert. We arrived at the Furnace Creek Inn, Death Valley, just in time for dinner that night. The rain had been left behind in another world. The Mohave Desert is dry, but compared with Death Valley it may be said to be wettish. Death Valley is one of the dryest and hottest regions in the world. Four hundred square miles of it lie well below sea-level, and in summer they must be like a gigantic frying-pan. Even at Furnace Creek, in a stand-ard-instrument shelter, the thermometer has gone up to 134° F and, as the official Guide remarks austerely, "out on the salt beds, without benefit of shade, it un-doubtedly is much higher." August on those salt beds, with no shade or water for miles, must be as near hell as you can get on this earth. The enormous valley, which is ringed around with high mountains, owes its sinister name to a party of 'Forty-niners who were trying a short cut to the gold mines and found their way into this terrible arid bowl. There they had to stay, with death hovering over them, until the scouts they sent out returned to lead them out of the valley over the mountains. Later, many prospectors came here looking for gold, and up in the mountains there are several ghost mining towns, such as Skidoo, Rhyolite, Bullfrog, and Panamint City. We went up to Bullfrog and Rhyolite once, through Hells Gate and over Daylight Pass, and found deserted streets, railway stations, hotels, saloons, cabins, all silent in the mountain sunlight. There was just one inhabitant, who sold souvenirs. His shanty had an elaborate little garden, but nothing was alive and growing there. He had made it out of old beer bottles, glittering quartz, tin foil, and the like: it was very quaint and ingenious, but rather sinister, like the last garden on a dead planet.

Death Valley is now a National Monument, which

means that it belongs to the people of the United States and is administered for their benefit by the National Park Service in a most admirable civilized manner. It has a magnificent winter climate, like that of the Arizona Desert, but rather warmer during the day. During the last forty years, a great deal of borax has been taken out of the Valley, and now the flourishing Borax Company has built a really fine large hotel there, the Furnace Creek Inn, which is open from the first of November to the first of May. It is astonishing to arrive at this hotel, standing there like a great stone fortress, but with palm gardens, a swimming-pool, tennis-courts, in the heart of this fantastic wilderness, hundreds of miles from anywhere. How they contrived to build such a large comfortable place, I cannot imagine, for every stone and stick in it must have had to be carted over mountain and desert. At the other end of the Valley, even farther from anywhere, really at the end of the earth, is the famous Death Valley Scotty's Castle, which must be the oddest private residence in the world. It is an ambitious building more or less Spanish in style, with hints of mediæval castles, toy forts, and palaces out of the *Arabian Nights,* and it has a carillon, and fountains, and portraits that light up, and has already cost millions and millions of dollars. Two partners own it: A. M. Johnson, who is said to be a millionaire from Chicago; and the famous Scotty, otherwise Walter Scott, an ex-cowboy and prospector, whose life for the last forty years is one tremendous legend. Years ago, long before he built his Castle, he once emerged, alone, from some mysterious part of the Valley, with bags of gold, and promptly chartered a special train to Chicago, two thousand miles away. I have heard that men used to follow him into the Valley, to try and locate his mines, but he always eluded them and then if they were not very careful they missed the few waterholes and died. All this has been happening in our time; you can go and see the Castle—and perhaps meet Scotty—for yourself; and yet it is all as mad as an Arabian fairy tale.

There are, the *Guide* tells us, no less than five hundred and twenty-eight species of wild plants in Death Valley, but if you go there in winter you do not seem to see any of them except the curious blanched desert-holly. It is the barest country you can imagine, all twisted out of rock, sand, and salt. Everything there is fantastic. From one viewpoint you see the highest point in the United States, the summit of Mount Whitney, and the lowest, the salt beds of the Bad Water area, nearly three hundred feet below sea-level. One part of the Valley floor, called the Devil's Golf Course, consists of miles of crystallized salt twisted into tiny pinnacles, hard as rock and so close together that you could not lay a book down flat there. The salt goes down for hundreds of feet. The mountain slopes show gigantic geological faults. Out of the Valley there run a number of narrow twisted canyons, and all their walls blaze with color. There are, too, some exquisite sand dunes. Nature here shows what she can do with a few simple materials, air and rock and sand, to create a rich beauty of both form and color. But to appreciate that beauty you must not be wondering, as the early travelers must often have wondered, if soon you would be lying on the sand and salt, swollen-tongued and black-faced under the pitiless sun. There could hardly be a better example than this of the way in which the comparative security and the amenities of civilization can change the situation. Two generations ago, this was one of the most sinister regions in America, as its name suggests. Now it seems almost an austere winter paradise, and a much better place to rest in than such resorts as Palm Springs. The great heights and depths, the many marvels, the enormous distances, the rainless air, the jeweled blaze of color, the glittering cold nights, these are ours now to enjoy; what was once Death Valley the menace, the fiery dragon across the path to California, is now Death Valley the National Monument, among the more precious possessions of the American people; and what once, not long ago, suggested death is now among the enchantments of life.

When we were not exploring the Valley, I explored the even more fantastic territories of Ouspensky's mathematical-mystical mind. To an Anglo-Saxon reader, he seems a queer mixture of scientific rationality and esoteric dogmatism. At one moment, he is patiently demonstrating his thesis on the lecture-room black-board, and the next moment he has put on the insignia of some strange mystical order and is being oracular before the altar. In England and America we tend to associate all talk of "esoteric doctrine" with companies of nice, arty, silly middle-aged women, busy feeling good and superior and having only the vaguest notion of what they are talking about. On the other hand, we expect a man who has had a good scientific education to be very wary of mysticism. But the old Russia liked to mix things up in people. One of its greatest composers was a chemist, another was an admiral. I feel that Ouspensky is very much a product of that old Russia. His thought is half-European, half-Asiatic. He knows an enormous lot about everything, but would not be recognized as an authority on any subject. He is not quite a scientist, not quite a philosopher, not quite a mystic, and yet seems all of a piece. Just when you feel he has embarked you with him on a stream of nonsense, he startles you into close attention by making a profoundly original observation or by plunging into a passage of brilliant reasoning. He has the gift of charming easy exposition: even in translation it shines through. I recognized in his work many of the traits I remembered noticing in Orage, who was at one time among his disciples: but he has a stronger and more original mind than Orage had. Such a man will never be officially welcomed as a philosopher, and I do not imagine that he wants to be thought a prophet or a high priest, so that we have no exact term of description for him. But the effect of his work is—at least to my mind—immensely stimulating. The darkness is being temporarily illuminated, if only by a series of rockets.

It was his chapters on Time, of course, that held me. Apparently he is an old Fourth Dimension enthusiast because he published a book on it nearly thirty years ago, which suggests that he took his own line very early in life. I found his theories of Time very confusing but almost intoxicating in their wealth of stimulating ideas. Unlike Dunne, whom he never mentions and who was obviously unknown to him when he wrote these chapters, he does not believe in a regressive series of Times. He believes that Time, like Space, has three dimensions, and only three. This means that the universe has six dimensions, of which the first three are recognized by us as being extended in Space, the fourth we call Time, and the fifth and sixth are unknown to us. He suggests that the fifth dimension, at right angles to the fourth if we are trying to think geometrically about them, will be Eternity, not ordinary Time extended to infinity, but timelessness, the perpetual existence of every moment along the line of the fourth dimension, the eternal Now. When we say the Past exists, it must exist along this dimension. But what then is the sixth dimension, the final third dimension of what we call Time? He does not give it a name, but says it is the line of the actualization of other possibilities contained in any moment but not actualized in our Time. This is difficult, but not totally incredible. He points out with some truth that so far as Time is concerned, we are one-dimensional creatures, analogous with the one-dimensional creatures of Space who would have to spend their whole existence along one line and know nothing beyond it. This is true of us intellectually. We are compelled to think of the single track of Time. But intuitively and in imagination we are not so narrowly bound. In high moments of emotion we seem to feel the timelessness, the eternal Now, of that fifth dimension. And dimly in imagination we may have some sense of that sixth dimension, that actualization of other possibilities.

It may be—I am theorizing now, not Ouspensky—that the imagination, a very mysterious faculty, not yet pinned down and labeled, is our first dim sense of this final dimension, movement along which would be creation. If we were free to move as we wished along the fourth and fifth dimensions, we could experience the Past. If we were given the freedom of this sixth dimension, we could change the Past, as an artist may change his work to bring it nearer to perfection. I seemed to remember something of this kind being suggested by Douglas Fawcett in his *World as Imagination*. Ouspensky arrives near this point, later in his book, when he suddenly produces the novel theory that the only possible reincarnation, and that only for a few highly-developed personages, is *into the Past*. Evil produces more evil, he argues, and therefore it must be checked at its source. According to this theory, then, the only way to clean up this present age would be for some noble being to reincarnate from the Future into our age and to labor from 1900 to 1914 to prevent the coming Great War. All this, of course, is the wildest nonsense on any conventional view of Time. The war and all the other evils have happened, and there is an end of it. The moving finger writes. But Ouspensky would say that the moving finger goes on writing the same thing over and over again, and can be induced to change a word or two.

This brings us to his strangest notion, one that haunted me like a queer dream just after I read his account of it in Death Valley. He holds that Time has a wavelike movement, that the line of the fourth dimension is circular. We think of Time and life running along a straight line, on which the birth and death of any person could be indicated by two points, the length of line between them being the life of that person. That is an illusion, according to Ouspensky. Our Time is far more personal than that. It may coincide to some extent with other Times, those of other people, the greater Time of the race or the world, but it is our own. There cannot be any of this Time for us outside the circle of it that we open at birth and close at death. The movement around and around this circle is Eternity. When a man dies, he immediately enters the same life from the other end, is born again in the same house, of the same parents, on the same day and year, and everything will happen as before. The only difference, he argues, is that there may be an inner development one way or the other. Some people, those comfortable creatures of custom we all know, live identically the same lives over and over again. Others, such as madmen, suicides, criminals, go through the same tragic performance with a dwindling inner life until at last there is nothing vital left in them. The conquerors march and fight and proclaim their triumphs over and over again. It is easier each time for Napoleon to win Austerlitz and Jena and to lose Leipzig and Waterloo. Popular novelists and such trash—for Ouspensky has no opinion of us—find success waiting for them at the same point along the track, and are increasingly corrupted by it. A few, the esoteric *élite*, learn to live, evolve properly, and so finally, in some mysterious fashion, turn the circle into a spiral, and escape. Ouspensky's treatment of this repellent theory of eternal recurrence is one of his best pieces of writing. There is a wealth of deeply imaginative illustration. I remember feeling enormously stimulated by it, with creative excitement mounting in me as I read. And at odd times ever since I have struggled with a play on the theme of this recurrence, and have done three complete versions already and do not like any of them. But

[275]

I did not find Ouspensky's theory satisfying. He made it do too much. It is both eternal and yet not eternal, for on his own showing it comes to an end for many people. If it can come to an end, it must have had a beginning. When were we all set going on this merry-go-round of existence? How many times already have I written this sentence? And if there is the smallest change whatever, the difference of the flicker of an eyelash, then we cannot be going over the same track of Time. If people show the least alteration, inward or outward, then these lives of theirs are no more recurrent than they are eternal. What are they, then? He does not tell us.

It seemed to me that he was equally stimulating and more satisfying in his earlier chapter, on the dimensions of Time. It gave me a glimpse of a universe that was as vast and subtle a conception as a universe ought to be. It has always seemed to me incredible that we should find ourselves part of a scheme of life that even to us appeared childish and arbitrary. Probably it is one of the weaknesses of our time that so many people feel that they have certain subtle states of mind to which nothing outside themselves can respond, as if they were poets who had been told they were part of a steam-engine. This universe of Ouspensky's is at least grand, rich, mysterious. I applauded him when I found him blandly dogmatic on a point that had entered my own vague and rather wistful speculations.

It is this. For a long time now the astronomers have described to us the terrible emptiness of space, in which the suns and circling planets are like a few peas thrown across Paddington Station. But this is merely to take a three-dimensional cross-section of the planetary systems, which are actually so many elaborately interwoven spirals. If we ourselves were sufficiently enlarged, these spirals might present to us hard surfaces and appear impenetrable. Those immense spaces would have vanished. Science itself admits this is possible because it tells me that the table on which I am now writing is mostly empty space. A particle of matter is not unlike a miniature solar system. Our idea of the stars and our idea of the atoms are both conditioned by our own size, which also enters into our perception of dimensions. Giant suns appear to us as points, without dimension. If we begin to theorize about the atom, at the other end of the scale, even four dimensions will not satisfy us. There may be much wild speculation here, but it is evident that, to say the least of it, we are living in a very strange complicated universe, not at all like the colossal steam-engine that our scientific grandfathers showed their startled clergy. And its six dimensions may well have the character, for us, that Ouspensky says they have.

This seemed to me his most fertile and satisfying thought. What we call Time or the fourth dimension is the line of actualization of a number of possibilities.

The fact that at certain moments there are many different possibilities is one that has always fascinated me, and I once wrote a play on the theme called *Dangerous Corner*, in which the characters took one line and then returned to where they started from and finally took another line. The fifth dimension considered in temporal terms might easily be, as he suggests, the infinite extension of all present moments, the Eternal Now. And I find something deeply attractive in the idea of a sixth dimension that is in effect the final thickness of all things, the welcome reply of the universe to our creative imagination. Movement along this last dimension would mean the actualization of all possibilities, the possible changing of the Past, the production in the end of the perfect drama of this or any other lives. I remembered sitting on deck late one night in the middle of the Pacific, when the wireless officer was talking casually about the passengers he had known. "We had a professor here once," he remarked idly, "who told me that it might be possible for a number of people, working together, to change the Past." That was all. I never learned who this professor was or how he thought this miracle could be performed. But it is strange how the thoughts of men, linked in Time but widely separated in Space, will begin to wander and stray and then run all in one direction. Along what dimension do they travel?

I think I knew then, even while I was staring, half

bewildered, half entranced, at *A New Model of the Universe*, with the desert of Death Valley around me like a very old model of this world, that I would never write my little book on Time. I did not know enough. I had not the right kind of mind, because, as every new and fascinating idea presented itself, this mind of mine did not carefully consider it but immediately conjured it into strange new tales and dramas. Apparently I could not resist running up and down the sixth dimension. If there was one, and this was not all moonshine. But why, I said to myself, should I not believe in this enchanting universe of many dimensions, in which we shall come at last, after much conflict and sorrow, to work everything out right, as we try to do in our novels and plays? If some of my friends speak the truth when they tell me that we only exist for a brief period, reproduce our kind, and are obliterated by death, then it only means that one night I shall go to bed still exploring this enchanting universe of many dimensions, then fall asleep in it forever. If they are right, I shall not wake from that sleep to go on exploring my universe, but I shall never know that they were right and I was wrong, and during my midget life under the sun I shall have known a better universe than they do or than nature and reality know how to make. *Give me my robe, put on my crown; I have immortal longings in me.*

Chapter Fourteen

THAT was all very fine, I said to myself as I crammed the typewritten sheets into the stove and watched weeks of work flare and vanish, that was all very fine, but you merely played with a few odd ideas and struck a few attitudes, and nothing really happened inside. What did you feel? What are you feeling now, after you have retraced the steps that took you from Santa Barbara and Death Valley to the fourth, fifth, and six dimensions? You are still, my fine dimension-juggler, feeling a little lost, a little bewildered, vaguely unhappy. You are, you know, in spite of all your broad comedy and your bounce and bluff, a Romantic, for even yet you don't live cunningly in the present tense and balance this pleasure against that, neatly inducing hunger and thirst so that you can enjoy the excellent food, the carefully chosen wine. No, you still shovel up and burn the common hours as you wait impatiently for the high moment, the Pisgah sight, the lifting of the veil, the dream coming through the multitude of business. At heart you are one with all those fools who see life as so many mountaineers must see Switzerland, that is, unendurable, not to be borne for an hour, if it were not for its shining peaks. You do not seem to be close to any summit at present. Your mind is sober and it's wishing it could be drunk again. When will be the next time, and what high moment is on its way? I couldn't answer this. But now both question and answer came together. When and where was the last high moment? It was during our recent trip to the Grand Canyon and while we were on the floor of the Canyon. Both selves agreed, became one again, and remembered.

This was not our first visit to the Grand Canyon. I plunged farther into recollection, and arrived at that first visit. We had planned "a stop-over" of a few hours. Your coach leaves the main west-bound train at Williams, Arizona, wanders up the sixty-four miles to the station at the Southern Rim of the Canyon, doing this during the night when you are fast asleep, and when you wake in the morning—there you are. That is the theory of this "side trip." It did not work well for me in practice. The night that had seemed very convenient and comfortable in the railway time-table was actually most unpleasant. First there were giant shuntings and bangings that made sleep impossible. By the time I had adapted myself to these shuntings and bangings, they stopped, and the train was left paralyzed in an uneasy silence and stillness, a doomed train that whispered, "Sleep no more." In the end I must have slept a little, for I remember waking to find that we were somewhere very high and it was snowing. Heavy and hot about the eyes, I put on some clothes, then went blinking and shuffling out into the cold blue morning, a peevish passenger.

The little station looked dreary. The young man waiting with the hotel bus did not look dreary, but he looked all wrong, for he wore a ten-gallon hat and an embroidered cowboy coat with English riding-breeches and long boots, like a cowboy in a musical comedy. The bus turned two corners and landed us at the front door of an hotel that was so tremendously Western that it might have been created by a German scene-designer who had never been farther west than Hamburg. I felt grumpy about all this. A lot of nonsense. The interior of the hotel took my breath away, not because it was very beautiful, but because it was overheated and seven thousand feet above sea-level. I continued to disapprove of everything, but condescended to eat a large breakfast. After breakfast it was still snowing a little and there was nothing to be seen through the hotel windows but snowflakes and mist. I went panting up and downstairs several times, a man in a temper with a large breakfast getting at him, and then very soon it stopped snowing, so I went out. A few paces in front of the hotel there were some seats, a low wall, and then nothing. The world did not extend beyond that wall. Apparently it was a flat world, after all, and here was the edge. I stared over these battlements and saw a few last snowflakes fall into misty space. I walked a few paces through the slush, moving parallel with the wall, and it was wet and raw and there was nothing more to see. I might have been standing on the Thames Embankment on a foggy morning, except that the misty nothing over the edge here had a vaguely illimitable look about it. I decided that I had had enough of this. I threw a last glance over the wall, and then, down there somewhere, there was a swirling, a lifting, a hint of some early creative effort in the mist of Time. The next moment what breath I had left was clean gone. I was looking into the Grand Canyon.

Once I had made sure it really was like that, I hurried back to the hotel, shouted the good news, arranged to stay on, and canceled the seats we had booked in the next train. There was to be no thought of trains. Even this one misty glimpse told me that a miracle had happened. At last, in all my travels, I had arrived and there had been no anticlimax, and my imagination, after weeks or months of expectant dreaming, had not cried, "Is that all?" Reality, stung by my many jeers at its poverty, had gone to work to show me a thing or two. I thought I could imagine a better Grand Canyon, did I? Well, cried Reality, take a look at this—and—oh boy! —you ain't seen nothing yet.

It juggled with all kinds of weather for us during that first short stay. We saw snow falling into that vast gulf, saw clouds stream below us, looked down on thunderstorms, stared at Nineveh and Thebes, rusty in the sunlight, coming through the mists, and watched rainbows arch and brighten and fade over the Painted Desert. We seemed to be witnessing, within a few hours, all the mad prodigality of Nature. One stupendous effect was piled on another; veils of mist and broken rainbows were caught in forests hanging in midair; the sunlight far below fell on ruined red cities; and to one hand, across the gulf, was a vertical Egypt, and to the other a perpendicular Assyria. There was in this immensity, although the weathers of four seasons and several climates seemed to chase one another down there, a silence so profound that soon all the noises from the life about us on the Rim were lost in it, as if our ears had been captured forever, drowned in these deeps of quiet. We had only to walk a few hundred yards to find ourselves staring at new gigantic vistas, more forests hanging in the mists, more temples crumbling in the sunlight, more rosy peaks, green chasms, and cloud shadows like wandering stains. But it is useless to try to describe the Grand Canyon. Those who have not seen it will not believe any possible description; and those who have seen it know that it cannot be painted in either pigments or words.

I have heard rumors of visitors who were disappointed. The same people will be disappointed at the Day of Judgment. In fact, the Grand Canyon is a sort of landscape Day of Judgment. It is not a show place, a beauty spot, but a revelation. The Colorado River, which is powerful, turbulent, and so thick with silt that it is like a saw, made it with the help of the erosive forces of rain, frost, and wind, and some strange geological accidents; and all these together have been hard at work on it for the last seven or eight million years. It is the largest of the eighteen canyons of the Colorado River, is over two hundred miles long, has an average width of twelve miles, and is a good mile deep. It is the world's supreme example of erosion. But this is not what it really is. It is, I repeat, a revelation. The Colorado River made it, but you feel when you are there that God gave the Colorado River its instructions. It is all Beethoven's nine symphonies in stone and magic light. Even to remember that it is still there lifts up the heart. If I were an American, I should make my remembrance of it the final test of men, art, and policies. I should ask myself: Is this good enough to exist in the same country as the Canyon? How would I feel about this man, this kind of art, these political measures, if I were near that Rim? Every member or officer of the Federal Government ought to remind himself, with triumphant pride, that he is on the staff of the Grand Canyon.

This incredible pageantry of sunlight and chasm, I thought, is our nearest approach to fourth-dimensional scenery. The three dimensions are on such a scale that some of the fourth has been added. You do not see, hung before you, the seven million years that went to the making of these walls and their twisted strata, but

[285]

you feel that some elements of Time have been conjured into these immensities of Space. Perhaps it is not size nor the huge witchery of changing shapes and shades that fill us with awe, but the obscure feeling that here we have an instantaneous vision of innumerable eons. There must be the profoundest of silences there because all the noises made throughout these years have no existence in this instantaneous vision of the ages, in which the longest time that any individual sound could take would be represented by the tiniest fraction of an inch on these mile-high walls.

Strangely enough—and now I am not being fanciful —the only certain example I have of that fourth-dimensional element in dreams, which I described in my account of Dunne's theory, is concerned with this Grand Canyon. After I had spent several hours, staring at it from various viewpoints, I had a growing feeling that I had seen it before. Those exquisitely shadowed reddish pinnacles and domes and towers were vaguely familiar to me. True, I had seen photographs and possibly a picture or two; but as every fellow visitor will agree, the Canyon landscape has a unique and indescribable quality. It was significant, too, that I had not expected to see what I did see, and it was only after I had spent some time looking at it that I began to ask myself why I should feel that somehow once before I had stared at this scene and more or less as I was doing it now, across and down from some high place. Then at last I remembered. Some years before I had had a dream that, unlike nearly all my dreams, had remained in my memory. In this dream I had found my way into an empty theater, one of those colossal and monstrous dream buildings, like the nightmare prisons that Piranesi drew. This theater was so high I could not see the roof, and its tiers of balconies were so broad that they came out of darkness and ran into darkness again. I had climbed up to one of the highest of these balconies, and now looked across the great dark gulf of the building towards the stage. But there was no stage in the ordinary sense, no proscenium, no platform, no curtains. What I saw there was real landscape, and I seem to remember feeling that this was not strange, considering the fabulous wealth and influence of this theater. But the scene itself was quite strange to me, had some of the bright rock-coloring of Egypt and yet was not Egyptian. Now, looking at the Grand Canyon, I knew what I had seen, years before, in that dream. I had—and have—no doubt about it. You may say that my dreaming gaze made a prodigious leap through space, catching a glimpse of the Canyon, half the world away. But I prefer to believe, with Dunne, that the self who stood on that theater balcony had an eye that moved along a Time dimension, not a spatial one, and went forward years, in a second, to share with my future waking self one of the moments I would spend staring down at the Canyon from the South Rim. Possibly there was something in the quality of this experience that lay along my Time One scale in the direction of the Future, that attracted the attention of my dreaming self, my Observer Two, and made him telescope into this dream, as a fitting spectacle for this greatest of all theaters, a glimpse of the most awe-inspiring landscape in the world. Certainly, nothing I had seen or experienced before in America matched this first sight of the Grand Canyon. I felt that God had set it there as a sign. Of what, I didn't know: I made no intellectual response to this challenge. But as I peered over the far edge of all familiar things, and I saw the storm clouds roll and flash in the gulf below, the rainbows tangled in the hanging woods, the sunlight turning the mist to drifting smoke and the vast shadowy walls into ruined empires, I kept muttering to myself that it had been set there as a sign. I felt wonder and awe, but at the heart of them a deep rich happiness. I had seen His handiwork, and I rejoiced.

Now this winter we had gone up there again, all of us this time, by road from the ranch. We filled two motor-cars, with a cowboy at each wheel. After leaving Prescott, we turned away from the main road, zigzagged fearfully among the mountains, and then dropped down into Oak Creek Canyon, where the storekeeper at Sedona was astonished to find his grocery counter suddenly besieged by six English children (all in tattered blue jeans, their parents and their nurse, and two grinning cowboys, demanding bread, butter, meat, cheese, fruit, chocolate, beer, and lemonade. He would have been even more astonished if I had told him that, in my opinion, he and his son and the old-timer smoking his pipe in the far corner were all living in Turner's vision of the Garden of the Hesperides. Oak Creek is Arizona turned idyllic. Here the mountains have married the desert, and their union has been most fruitful. At one moment you are among the firs and the ice-cold waterfalls, and the next moment you are looking down again on sand and cactus. It is said that on one forty-acre lot in Oak Creek you may find firs and figs, trout and cactus, mountain pines and tobacco plants, desert sand and roses. If you filmed the extravagant place, you would be accused of impudent and careless faking. When we ate our lunch there, outside that astonished store, the valley was filled with an exquisitely soft gold sunshine. The hillsides were fresh and green. There was the happy noise of running water everywhere. Around the floor of the canyon, very sharp and bright in the sunlight, were great twisted shapes of red sandstone, looking like ruined fairy-tale castles and mysterious monuments. It was all strangely beautiful, very remote but very friendly, like some place not quite in this world, a lost happy valley in some antique tale. I felt like saying that at last we had arrived in Avalon and must stay here forever, vanishing from the world that had known us. Why go on? Why make plans and consult time-tables

[289]

and go on and on when we could sit in the shade of these great oaks and "fleet the time carelessly as they did in the golden world"? Here within a morning's walk were all the climates worth having, with the Highlands of Scotland and Canada within waving distance of Africa and Australia, and the children who were tired of the warm sand and the prickly cactus could go and find fir cones in the snow. And yet this place was not a little bit of everything neatly assembled, but was itself and unique. These giant red sculptured rocks, like the last ruins and monuments of the oldest city in the world, gave the green valley a charm as deeply romantic as that of any South Sea islands I had seen, and it had none of their failings, their clammy messiness, their monotonous sighing palms, their eternal flavorless afternoons. Here was the perfect haven. Why go on?

But after lunch, off we went, corkscrewing over more mountains, plunging into winter again, and in the early dark of that night we arrived at the new Lodge on the South Rim. Its welcome was warm and liberally laced with the smell of pine logs and varnish. The waitresses and the few other guests in the dining-room were entertained by the sight of our rosy English cheeks and tattered jeans and by the splendor of our appetites. The next morning, after arranging to take the older children with us and our two cowboy guides down into the Canyon, we discovered Bernard Shaw and Mrs. Shaw, who had just arrived from San Francisco with a party from a cruise ship. That miraculous elder had just spent two nights in a train, and there he was, at eighty, as pink and bright-eyed as ever, ready to look at anything, go anywhere, contradict anybody. We had known him in England, but the children hadn't, and I found a special pleasure in presenting them to the great and indestructible G.B.S. To meet the Grand Canyon and Bernard Shaw on the same morning—what an adventure! Then the children went rambling along the Rim, and were constantly being photographed by the people of the cruise party, who all thought they had found some genuine young raggle-taggle Westerners and were drolly surprised when they learned, after a question or two, that these picturesque youngsters came from London, too. There was a bookstall in the hotel and I wanted something to take with me into the Canyon, so I had a look at it. Once again the little miracle happened. The very first row of books I saw were novels that had been reduced in price because nobody wanted them. There under my hand was a translation of Franz Kafka's *The Castle*, a novel I had been wanting to read for some time. I knew then that everything was all right, that for a little while the stars were on my side. Into the kit-bag, with my pajamas and toothbrush and slippers, went *The Castle*. Off we went, four excited children, two vaguely apprehensive parents, and the two cowboy guides, fine young fellows, several miles along the Rim, past snowy pine woods and peeping deer, to the head of the Kaibab Trail.

Here it was that I was first introduced to a creature that is now a character in our family epic. If ever since that day I have been called upon to draw some gigantic bus, airplane, ship, or castle for the younger children, and to show us all enjoying ourselves in the fantastic vehicle or dwelling, then I have had to include this creature. He is part of the domestic legend. He was— and I hope still is—a very large white mule, the largest of the trail mules, specially created by an all-wise Nature to carry my formidable bulk and weight up and down seven thousand feet. His name was Marble. He had two tricks that distinguished him from the other mules and brought him immortality. When he came to a sharp turning in the horribly narrow trail he did not sidle and shuffle around it at once, as the others did, but leaned forward so that his head and neck and shoulders were in midair and his unhappy rider was wondering how soon he would be pitched into the precipice. Sometimes, with shocking malice, he would slowly lower his head over the dreadful edge, so that I would find myself clinging to the saddle-horn and looking down several thousand feet. His second trick was that he would suddenly stop on the trail and try to eat something. Anything would do, vegetable or mineral; he was the coarsest and craziest of feeders; and we began to invent gluttonous feats for him, until in the end we decided that it was Marble who had eaten out most of the Grand Canyon. I spent three days in the company of this strange monster, and came to have a kind of exasperated affection for him, like that of a wife for an incorrigible husband.

Perched gigantically, then, on Marble, I followed the others and found myself descending the south wall of the Canyon. The Kaibab is a new trail that appears to have been blasted and scraped out of the vast rock faces, and there has never been a serious accident on it. After the first half-hour, I began to enjoy it, but during that first half-hour I kept wondering which of us would be hurled first into the rocky gulf. We descended through one geological age after another, and as the afternoon wore on, the very climate changed. The Canyon itself lost nothing of its awful immensity. New chasms and precipices, with richly stained walls, came into view, and behind us the rock face, with great trees that now looked like tiny bushes, climbed to the sky. The trail would go forward to a spur, beyond which was a huge space and a simmering reddish vision of a vertical desert. Into that space the malevolent Marble would push his idiot head while the others, having safely turned the corner, would look back and up and laugh. The cowboys, who had mounted themselves on young fresh mules, would cavort on the edge of nothing, and shout bad jokes to one another and to the children, who were in a slithery, dusty paradise. There was a great deal of dust now and we were in full summer, apparently a thousand miles away from the snowy Rim. The Colorado River, which had looked like a length of string from the top, now seemed a fair-sized stream. The Canyon went up and up, but it also still went down and down. Whole tracts of it invisible from above suddenly arrived, to be zigzagged down for the next half-hour or so. Nothing in this descent diminished the size of the Canyon by so much as an inch. It lost no impressiveness. On every hand it opened out into new marvels of form and color; there was no end to it; what had seemed like dim ruined temples from above now towered as separate sunset-colored peaks, as if a whole mountain range had been tumbled into the vast chasm. But now we had left the sculptured red rocks above and behind us and were sliding dustily down rough tracks of limestone. The Colorado had turned into a menacing broad flood, thick and heavy, like dirty cream. It carries so much silt in it that if a man falls in, his clothes are so heavily saturated that he sinks at once. We could see a suspension bridge over to our right, and immediately below us was the entrance to a tunnel in the rock. This tunnel brought us straight on to the bridge and we went swinging high above the sinister Colorado.

Once across the river, fairly at the bottom of the Canyon, I felt not only that expansion which follows accomplishment, but also a sense of deep satisfaction and peace. It was warm down here—and by this time we were all very dusty, hot, and rather tired—but it was beginning to look green and fresh. We went along the bank of the great river a little way, turned a corner, and passed a camp occupied by the fortunate young men of the C.C.C. who worked in the Canyon, chiefly at keeping the trails in good order. I call them fortunate because winter was six thousand feet above them, they could sit in the sun, they had some decent work to do for the good of their own community, and they were being reasonably well sheltered and fed and paid in one of the most enchanting places on earth. And when I remembered that these brown, husky lads who waved at us were the new American equivalent of the unemployed English youths who stand outside our labor exchanges and at slushy street corners, just miserably kept alive by the dole, I could not see that we could teach the Americans much about social services. It seemed to me, however, that unemployment in this southwest could never be the drab tragedy it is with us, because here there is the sun, and it can never be so hopeless doing nothing and eating little in this sunlight as it is in the rain and sleet. If ever I have to endure neglect and poverty, I thought, I hope I am given sufficient warning so that I can at least crawl into the sunshine, where I shall need less shelter, fuel, food, and clothes, and can at least be warm when I sit and remember past happiness. So, as I jogged rather wearily by the camp on Marble, who seemed as indifferent about ending the journey as he had been about starting it, I felt a sudden deep compassion for my own people, six thousand miles away in the cold rain and fog, and was disturbed by a vague uneasiness, as if my conscience whispered that I should not be here, happy in the sun, when they were still there, in an England that had long ceased to be merry for most of them.

I saw something then, however, that whisked away that uneasiness, and made me want to cry aloud my happiness. This was our lodging for these next two days, Phantom Ranch. It had an orchard bright with blossom. To come at the end of this fantastic journey, hours of rock and dust and giant stone shapes, to this little green place and to find it snowing blossoms there, like May in Hereford, was an enchanting experience. We went to our cabins, washed off the dust and quenched our thirst, then separated, to go birding, to explore, to splash in the stream, in the last hour of full daylight left us. Phantom Ranch is at the entrance to Bright Angel Creek, its bright angel being the clear stream of good drinking water that refreshed the early explorers. It is a beautiful side-canyon, with high narrow twisting walls, exquisitely green along the banks of the stream. There I went strolling, up the Creek, feeling a little sore and stiff after those hours with Marble, but expanded, at ease, and for once in a restless life, at peace. Before I had gone very far, moving slowly, almost luxuriously, and lighting my pipe, the sunlight had crept away from the green depths of the creek and was now high on the walls, lighting up their russet and bronze faces. As I went forward, there came into my view up to the right a magnificent great half-dome of rock, full in the sunlight, and deep gold against the sky. The long descent, the sudden vision of the blossom, the clear running stream, the bluebirds and goldfinches flashing in the green dusk, and now this tremendous sun-crowned rock! Yet it was not the beauty of the place or the hour, though they were beautiful, that I remembered best, but the peace of mind, the peace of heart, I felt as I walked there. Something was due to the mere sense of accomplishment, even though I had done no more than any elderly woman with good nerves and the dollars to spend might accomplish. Something was due to the sense of physical well-being after the exercise I had taken. Perhaps, too, a certain release and expansion after having left Marble and finding myself still whole, for I may have been more apprehensive deep down than I thought I was. And if I am at heart a Romantic, then this tiny green valley a mile deep and almost in another world, possibly satisfied some hunger of my spirit. So much must be allowed, and to it must be added the sunset loveliness of the scene.

Yet there was something more, some deeper satisfaction still, came then to bring that peace. Remembering our time down there at Phantom Ranch, there returned a series of little pictures: the vast happy-family meals we had in the ranch dining-room; the noisy round games we played with the cowboys afterwards in the recreation room ("Best and liveliest bunch we ever had down here," they said, and we knew that the family had been awarded its highest decoration); the ride up through the narrowing Creek to Ribbon Falls and the picnic there; the deep indigo nights with so many stars hidden by the vast darkness of the Canyon walls; my midnight hours in my cabin with Kafka's book, a journey from this strangeness of the Canyon floor to the further strangeness of Kafka's allegorical world, with its tormented land-surveyor hurrying through the dark snowy village streets, trying to find somebody who will admit him into the mysterious Castle, with its vision of bewildered and blundering humanity looking for divine grace, in a tale entrancingly shaped and as haunting as a clear dream, yet with something in it alien and vaguely repellent to me.

All this and more came back to me now, yet the little walk I had up the creek that first evening remained the dominant memory and I found myself constantly returning to it. I remembered very little of what I must have seen, which is one more proof that I am not naturally very observant. I could not recall what I had been thinking about during the walk, and I suspected, on that account, that for once that busy upper level of my mind, the professional department with its themes and topics and smart debating points, had given itself a holiday. No, all that remained was the quality of that hour, the deep satisfaction, the peace. My memory clung to it as if every step I had taken along that path had been set to exquisite music. The time value was queer, perhaps significant. It lasted hardly any ordinary time at all, at most an hour, yet though I cannot fill its space in my memory with any details of what I saw and thought and felt, it seems to have had more real time in it than some whole years of hurrying and scurrying I have had. Or you can say, with equal truth, that it had a timeless quality; there were no ticking clocks gnawing it away. It is almost like a remembered little life, and a perfect one. As that great half-dome of rock summit brightened to gold and then slowly faded to bronze, was stone and then fire and then stone again, some old hunger of the spirit was fed at last, and I was refreshed and at peace. That I was alone was a mere physical accident, for I do not think the experience came out of solitude and that the soul of it was solitary. It would have been just the same, I believe, if I had gone looking for birds or had idly splashed in the stream with the others. Though I happened to be alone, the others were in this with me, and had they not been there, had they not traveled and arrived as I had traveled and arrived, the experience would not have had this quality. Just as we had shared the trip, so too, I believe, on some mysterious rich deep level of feeling, we were still sharing. Thus the hour was immensely enriched.

There was much in this that I could not attempt to explain, I thought, as I leaned forward in my chair (for the fire in the stove was rapidly dying down), but I must try to make this last little bit clear to myself. Where exactly did I stand? I believed that only persons who could suffer or be glad, who alone knew values, really existed—that is, were alive on every possible level—in this world. Therefore, the question and test for everything must always be, What does it do to persons? If Man was not made for the Sabbath, then he certainly was not made for Debrett or the Social Register, Imperial Chemicals, Limited, the Standard Oil Company, the Party, the State. So I upheld the individual against the totalitarian State or any other machine—for all organizations are a kind of machine —that had somehow acquired the reputation of being more important than persons. Every age has its own peculiar perils, and ours seemed to be a tendency to believe in machines rather than in persons, to sacrifice what belonged to human personality to what belonged to mere machinery, so that the very people who began rebelling against some moloch-machine only ended by building another one themselves and sacrificing persons to it.

This did not mean that I distrusted all forms of co-operation, and was suspicious of what could be done by the Community. The community, unlike the State, is a total of persons as persons, and our life is rooted in it. Without the Community, we should live like brutes. The very people who sneered at it took a heavy toll of its services, without the ghost of a "Thank you." We are born heavily in debt to the Community, and if we make no effort to repay that debt, there is always something patched-up and furtive about our lives. Of all this, I was quite sure. On the first level of our life, the outward physical manifestation of being, although we appeared such separate thick lumps of flesh and bone, I believed with my friends, the philosophical biologists or biological philosophers, that our individual separateness was illusory. We are all tiny twigs on a tree, little lines in a vast pattern, brief conduits in a gigantic aqueduct; and for most of us, the more we make our outward lives conform to this idea of them, the happier we shall be. Thus there is health and sanity in any institution, such as the family, that expresses this idea. But to regard this biological progress as the whole of life, with whatever else you may value as so many mysterious "trimmings" on it, simply did not make sense to me. If I am told that I must accept some such view of things because, although it may hurt my vanity and chill my imagination, it represents the truth, I can only reply that I cannot see why such a short-lived brute of the earth as it makes me out to be should be asked to have any reverence for the truth. What's truth to me, on

[301]

this view of things, so long as I can fill my belly, keep warm, and enjoy my mate? In short, I believed that the very fact that these people were at some pains to employ their reason in order to convert others, proved that they were wrong and that they were leaving out of their account of life the better part of themselves, the very self who was at work.

Indeed, it seemed to me that on the next level, which is a whole vital world and not a collection of "trimmings," there was room and some urgent need for individuality. This was the level of the sciences and philosophies and arts, of experiencing, reflective, inventive, creative man. If there is not individual variety here, we perish or dwindle into bees and ants. That was why, in spite of my strong feeling of community and my belief in some form of collectivism, I was ready to fight for liberty not only of expression, my own particular professional interest, but also in the manner of living, which is itself a form of expression. Thus, the art and the style of life of a Chopin or a Duse are all of a piece, and we must not welcome one while condemning the other. Here, I thought, I am an individualist, yet I knew that if we try to make our individualism, glorious though it may be on this level of creation and appreciation, an end in itself, or find it impossible to see any farther, then a kind of hell waits to receive us. It is the lonely hell of the solipsist, but solipsism is merely a danger signal to most philosophers, and we have to look elsewhere to find it functioning as a private prison.

It is chiefly among letters and the arts that you discover those supreme individualists, the delicate experiencers, the experts of exquisite sensations, who come at last to know the taste of everything and the use and value of nothing. They go on tasting and escaping, retreating farther and farther, slowly backing into hell. They began well, but somehow and somewhere they had taken a turning into a blind alley. Nothing exists for them but a world of fine sensations and themselves, and even the fine sensations begin to fade. When such men have been writers, they have often written beautifully and with great penetration on many things, but there is always about their work—and it is more and more obvious as they get older—a suggestion of sterility, a growing desolation. The Sahara, we are told, is steadily eating its way towards the green heart of Africa, for desert if left unchecked creates more desert; and the more expensive bookshops are filled with limited signed editions of this desert work. It is individualism accepted so blindly and then so persistently cherished and refined that it turns stale, infertile, and begins to smell of death. There are nobler things in Proust, but there is more than a suggestion of this, too, and it desolates us as we read. We all know the work of such men, books that are like exquisitely written notes pushed to us from under the door of a cell of solitary confinement. No doubt

the walls of these cells are covered with the most entrancing mural decorations, but we who are outside
know that there is no life in them and that they only
feebly represent the vivid, warm, budding world.

The truth is that this second level of existence is no
more final than the first. We are complicated creatures
living in an extremely elaborate universe. Our mental
picture of it is even more over-simplified than a poster.
I had begun to understand that the messy little lino
cuts that popped in and out of my mind could give me
only the vaguest, tiniest hint of reality, that our ears,
only capable of picking out one of the oboes, could not
tell us that we are in the presence of a symphony orchestra. If this is a universe of many dimensions, as it
now appears to be, I felt there is something in us that
would come at last to explore and know them all. There
was room now for the grandest immortality, not an
endless and senseless going on and on in one direction,
but a complicated growth, forever adding new powers,
new responsibilities, new chances of disaster or triumph.
It might be, as I sometimes thought, that this life is
simply the creation of a fourth-dimensional body that,
when it is completely discovered to us, will begin to
move across a new field of Time, starting with the whole
content of its first life as a dramatist might start with
so many actors, costumes, scenes, and properties. On
the other hand, it might be that Dunne was right in
saying that we are already living in these farther times

and that only shadows and whispers of their existence come to us because our attention is rightly fixed on this immediate time. (Here I repeated my former argument in defense of such belief. If all this was moonshine, if life for us was quite simple and brutish: we are born, we see so many Springs, then we are completely extinguished; then not only could I never know I was wrong, but while alive I have lived in a richer universe than the one with the power of pronouncing my death sentence and of executing me; I have, in fact, created a better universe and lived my little life in it.) A belief in an immortality of this kind could repel with scorn the familiar Marxist charge of being "dope for the masses." There was no dope in it. No special rewards were promised by it for having been slave-driven in this world. (Though rationalist critics always seemed to me to miss the profound psychological truth of such observations as "The meek shall inherit the earth," for the meek, that is, those who are modest but hopeful in heart and mind, continually inherit the earth, for it is theirs to enjoy, whereas the proud, who expect everything, who are greedy, impatient, and dissatisfied, live in a rapidly diminishing world and soon enjoy nothing. As a man who could do with more meekness, I knew the truth of all this.) What happened here to you, on this theory of immortality, was of immense importance. It made life more rigorous and responsible, not less so. And it seemed to me to take no significance away from our ordinary outward life while giving a new significance to our inner life, which was not some vague bits and "trimmings," but part of a profoundly real existence, a first glimpse of our immortal adventure.

Such exits down strange corridors of Time, movements in unknown dimensions, suggested at first, I knew, that each of us goes forward alone, as solitary as the dreamer with his dream. But I soon saw that this could not be true. We do not even know for certain if the dreamer is solitary in his dream. Our apparent separateness, which is illusory on any level of life, probably does not even persist as an illusion on these further levels. You have only to add a dimension—the fourth to our ordinary three dimensional cross-section of things —to discover how our isolation vanishes, and what seemed a heap of branches, twigs, leaves, and fruit now appears as a growing tree. The more inward we go, the more we seem to overlap and share. Mind refuses to be isolated. We know now that some minds can communicate through no known channels of sense and can do it neatly to order to help Professor Rhine in his research. This is probably the grossest form of such communication, only a tiny illumination of the surface of a vast ocean of communing minds. Our life is a mystery; and it is significant that those cocksure facile reasoners who assure us that it is nothing of the kind can only return a blank stare to every fundamental question we ask about it. Probably in our ordinary physical life, which is taken to be the grand reality, we are only giving a sort of marionette performance of ourselves. Just as the marionettes, in a parody of communication, are completely separate entities, sharing little, when compared with the people who are coöperating behind the curtain to pull the strings and produce the little voices, so too this isolation we know is merely one of the conditions of the brief physical performance we give in its own little Space and Time. It is possible that when we assume we are most isolated, alone and awake at night, wandering solitary in thought, as I was doing in that Arizona hut, we are in reality least isolated, are not thinking and feeling by ourselves at all, have lost the hard outlines of our individuality, and only realize suddenly at times then that we are intensely alone because we keep awaking with a shock to the fact of our physical isolation. Either we are closer together in mind or spirit than we are aware of, share infinitely more than we can realize, or we live in a world of unanswerable questions. Why do minds widely separated in space begin to work on the same problems at the very same time? What has really happened to all those Romeos and Juliets whose whole lives are changed in an evening? Why do we seem to meet so many people for the first time in an atmosphere charged with attraction or repulsion? Where does inspiration come from? What is imagination, the strangest of faculties and yet the one most taken for granted? Why is it, age after age, men not without wisdom have compared themselves to actors playing parts, have been aware of another reality more fundamental and more closely shared —just as the mimic king and queen, courtiers and peasants, are all players back in the greenroom—than this brief brittle existence on the little lighted stage? If there is no invisible sphere, no great communion of mind, no shared adventures of the spirit, no reality unknown to outward sense, and all's plain sailing, why do we seem to move through a haunted world?

Chapter Fifteen

AND, I decided, I had been here in this hut quite long enough. It was ten minutes past midnight. I had been there about twenty minutes, and hadn't spent five of them really tidying up. Yet there was little left to do. The condemned chapters had been burned, and so had the Hollywood stuff and some notes and the letters I didn't want to keep. What was there left to keep, apart from my manuscript? Not much more than would go in a pocketbook. I caught myself feeling vaguely sad about this—though I would be the first to grumble if I was landed with an armful of imperishable souvenirs —and told myself not to be a fool.

Yawning, I went to the door, opened it, and switched off the light behind me. The night was immense, clear, and ice-cold after that smoky little hut. I should not have many more of these desert nights of stars. I was not sorry, because I am too restless to develop any loyalty even to a place I really enjoy, and I go away easily because I have not to pull at the least tendril of a root. I could drift rootlessly about the world, like the tumbleweeds I had seen down here. I am not proud of this. I was thinking as I picked my way past the

[309]

cholla and prickly pear that I should be healthier and stronger in mind, better able to set a course and stick to it, both more patient and more cunning in my art, if I could call a piece of countryside my own place and draw sustenance from its soil. But I was old enough to know that such is not my nature, and that though I may look every year more and more like a farmer or at least a seed merchant, I shall remain behind that massive disguise a sort of thin peddler or mountebank. I must suck what nourishment I can get out of the wind instead of drawing it richly from the soil, and at the very end I shall still be discovering what it is I want to do and planning the miraculous leap towards it. But if I cannot be loyal, I can be grateful. After I had carefully crossed the bars of the cattle-guard and had passed through the gate and was climbing up to the patio, I felt a sudden warmth of gratitude for this strange new-old country that had lent me all this winter its sun, its crystalline spaces, its amethyst mountains, its scarlet and blue birds, its huge nights of stars. I was too restless to settle down here or anywhere else, but I can always summon up enough patience to write a book. The pale walls and dark tiled roof of the patio were suddenly before me mysterious in the starlight. Yes, one day soon, I thought, I must try to put some of this into a book.

Set in Linotype Caslon Old Face
Format by A. W. Rushmore
Manufactured by the Haddon Craftsmen
Published by Harper & Brothers, New York and London